The Realities of Fiction

Books by Nancy Hale

❦

The Realities of Fiction

{A BOOK ABOUT WRITING}

by Nancy Hale

GREENWOOD PRESS, PUBLISHERS
WESTPORT, CONNECTICUT

Library of Congress Cataloging in Publication Data

Hale, Nancy, 1908-
    The realities of fiction.

    Reprint of the 1962 ed. published by Little, Brown,
Boston.
    1. Fiction--Authorship. I. Title.
[PN3355.H28 1977]   808.3   76-53839
ISBN 0-8371-9351-6

Originally published in 1962 by Little, Brown and Company,
Boston

Reprinted with the permission of Nancy Hale

Reprinted in 1977 by Greenwood Press, Inc.

Library of Congress Catalog Card Number   76-53839

ISBN 0-8371-9351-6

Printed in the United States of America

To John Ciardi

The author wishes to thank the following for permission to use copyrighted material:

Charles Scribner's Sons for an excerpt from "The Three-Day Blow" by Ernest Hemingway.

Harper & Row, Publishers for an excerpt from "The Door," in THE SECOND TREE FROM THE CORNER by E. B. White.

Harcourt, Brace & World, Inc. for an excerpt from A PASSAGE TO INDIA by E. M. Forster, copyright, 1924, by Harcourt, Brace & World, Inc.; renewed, 1952, by E. M. Forster. Reprinted by permission of Harcourt, Brace & World, Inc.

"A Passage to Relationship" appeared in the *Antioch Review;* "The Two-Way Imagination" (under the title "The Magic of Creativity") in the *Saturday Evening Post;* "The Other Side of the Cove" in *Poetry;* "Through the Dark Glass to Reality" (under the title "Through the Looking-Glass to Reality") and "How to Keep from Writing" in the *Saturday Review;* "Hemingway and the Courage to Be" in the *Virginia Quarterly Review.*

Contents

The Realities of Fiction

ONE

Introduction

MANY an author will speak of writing, in his best work, more than he actually knows. "I can't imagine where it came from," he will say. What are we to make of such an unearned wisdom? Psychologists have one sort of answer. I myself have always been pleased with a line from A. A. Luce's *Berkeley's Immaterialism*: "To say, then, that bodies subsist in the mind of God is to say that God is the home of the perceivable when it is unperceived by man." Through fiction, the hitherto unperceived may sometimes become perceivable. Somewhere between the New Critics' insistence upon viewing the work of literature in apartheid, and a purely biographical approach, lies the perception of the literary work as a symbol of its whole author — not, indeed, of the man as he wrote it, but of that man together with something hitherto hidden in him, here projected. It is not exactly he, this work of fiction; yet one cannot say that it is not he, either.

I am not, of course, talking about the exercise by which the psychiatric patient seeks to know himself more truly by going on at length on paper about whatever comes into his mind.

Such an exercise may prove of inestimable benefit to the patient, but it is not writing. It may do no actual harm to anybody else if some publisher chooses to print it, but it causes a dull aesthetic pain. The mechanism employed here to trap the wary complex in its lair has been called by one school of analysts "active imagination"; but, as W. H. Auden said when someone mentioned it, "What other kind is there?" There is a world of difference between writing inspired by therapeutic motives and writing that is done for the purpose of creating something of excellence. A work of art has to be written for itself, not for a reason.

However, just as the fiction-writer uses for material what other people have forgotten — the past, the meaning of the past — so does the finished work of fiction, when written wholly for itself without *arrière-pensées*, prove to have, when all is said and done, in turn its residue, the meaning of its meaning, the past within its past. All creations seem to me to be round and to have their outer and their inner curves. Behind the curve of the finished work of fiction, with all its diverse meanings for the world of readers, curves its meaning to the author himself — what, all the while he was addressing the world, he had to say to himself. Generally speaking, he won't listen. His secret (and as Yeats says, "The knowledge of reality is always in some measure a secret knowledge; it is a kind of death") is a secret he will not, cannot, tell himself or even his friends; only strangers — readers — receive his gift of wisdom. The real writer, otherwise such an apparent egotist, never writes of or for his own good. Yet writer after writer, it seems to me, sets down on paper knowledge that, if he were to help himself to it, would save him from tragedy. Such an ingestion

would naturally be the merest sequel to, by-product of, creation. But by it the writer, last and humblest at the feast which
he has set, might also partake.

The present volume is based on my past five years of lecturing on fiction at various institutions, and on the writing of
fiction at the Bread Loaf Writers Conference at Middlebury
College in Vermont. I do not subscribe to the notion that everybody can be taught to write (although I do believe that practically everybody has creative ability). Some people with an
acute urge to express something in words and a degree of confusion and timidity about how to do it can be helped to avoid
well-known technical pitfalls, or at least to recognize them
when they have fallen in, and to benefit by some well-known
devices for achieving the effects they want. Excitement about
writing is something else again, and can be transmitted, as can
enthusiasm about the value of writing as a way of life — even,
for a few, the very conception that writing can *be* a way of
life, instead of what a lady-president once described the work
I do as: an activity. If I can awake one spark of spontaneous excitement about writing, that is all the teaching I want to do.

All such boosts up the cliff to achievement must, I believe,
be given from underneath, behind, inside; by someone who
knows what it feels like to be a writer. In the course of lecturing I have attended a number of academic courses in what was
called in the catalogue "creative writing," and I couldn't see
that the painstaking analysis to which the professors subjected
famous works of fiction would be likely to teach anybody how
to do anything except to read with a more informed attention.
Fiction is never a work of analysis. It is a work of synthesis.

This book is also an attempt to show how much like the

requirements of real life the requirements of writing fiction are. For we might say that though the truths that emerge in fiction are not reality, are not the living truth, they are instead a John the Baptist to the coming reality. Fiction at its best can be a preparer of consciousness for the new being, a vaccinator against what would otherwise be too potent to endure. Just as time and again in literature's history fiction has prepared the world's mind for the political, social, or moral movings and shakings to come, so today, aided by understanding, not only readers but writers inclined to further development may also, by lending an uneasy ear, catch in fiction the voice of one crying in a wilderness of words. The writer in an existential world thus has the opportunity to unearth from his depths values which, perhaps uniquely, he can claim as his own.

TWO

The Two-Way Imagination

YEARS ago, when I was a young writer, I was planning a novel about the Paris of the Nineties, where my father was an art student. He used to tell me tales of his adventures there, and now they seemed to be taking a shape in my mind. But I had never been to Paris; and I asked my editor, Maxwell Perkins of Scribner's, if he would send me some books about the place and the period, so that I could bone up on it. He wrote back, sending me a couple of books, but urging me not to do too much reading. He warned me of the dangers of research to fiction. "You don't want to know too much about it," he said. "You want to make it up out of your head." He was quite right. The dead hand of research lies heavy on too many novels. The part most alive in them came out of the imagination.

But a few years after Perkins said that to me, while I was still young and foolish, I was foolish enough to say at a party, to a theologian and a sociologist, that my editor had told me not to know too much about what I was writing of. I'll never

Given as the 1960 Abernathy Lecture at Middlebury College.

forget the look on the faces of the sociologist and the clergyman. Having spent *their* entire lives trying to know as much as possible about what they were writing of, the clergyman looked at me as if I had blasphemed the Holy Ghost, and the sociologist looked most scientifically shocked. Yet both of them knew that I am a writer of fiction. And that is what fiction is: fiction, not fact.

Some people settle the whole question by deciding that everything in novels is just plain fact, after all. But I encounter a reproachful look, as though of betrayal, in the faces of friends who have *had* to realize that something they have read of mine was not true; never happened. A nice woman, wife of a clergyman in the town where I live, admired a story of mine which is written in the first person and called "The Empress's Ring." One day, I told her that I had never, in real life, possessed a ring that belonged to an empress; and that the ring I did own never got lost, as the one in the story did. I don't think she has ever felt quite the same about me since. Yet actually she had fair warning that the story was imaginary. It was labeled fiction in the book's blurb.

Maybe we are up against one of those things which today it is fashionable to call a dichotomy. On the one hand society, that is to say the reader, is continually being puzzled, upset, and betrayed by what fiction-writers do. The truth of the matter, however, is that society also expects fiction to persuade it into the willing — or even unwilling, the inadvertent — suspension of disbelief. The reader *wants* to believe in the novel, or else he wants his money back. He wants to identify with characters. He wants to live in the pages of the novel. But when he closes its covers at the end, he is often not resigned to the realization that none of it was true. He is like the little boy who wakes up from a dream that his pockets are full of gold, and hurries to the chair where he hung his pants last night, full of anticipation. Imagination is a kind of blind spot in the non-writing member of society. Because of course, everybody has imagination.

Indeed, there is a great deal of fault to be found with imagination. If you have the thought "Everyone hates me," or if you consider it a good idea to see what is the matter with the light fuse by poking your finger into the socket, or if you suppose that you can sail a boat because you have seen other people do it, or if you conclude that a friend has turned against you (when in fact her brusqueness was the result of not thinking about you at all) — those are all examples of an undisciplined imagination. It is obvious how dangerous such imaginings can be. The statistical dreamer in everyone, unrecognized, is one of the most dangerous forces on earth. Malicious gossip, which takes the place of creation in non-creative lives, of course draws heavily on imagination. Fear and superstition have their roots in imagination. The fact is that imagination is antisocial in that it is not in any relation at all to everyday reality. Let us see if we can catch a glimpse of what imagination is in relation to.

Probably because of such destructive phantasies as those I just listed, imagination hasn't a terribly good reputation in our society. Of course if I were to say that So-and-So was lacking in imagination, it would be understood as not a compliment. But if I call someone a dreamer, or say that someone has a head full of fancies, or say to someone, "That's all your imagination" — those are not compliments either. It might be objected that such disparagements apply to what one might call amateur dreamers, and that a novelist, for instance, ought to have a highly organized, well-disciplined, active imagination. Yet to say, "She certainly has a *lively* imagination" isn't praise either. That old phrase "nothing but imagination" is one of the commonest, one of the most damning, in use today. I would point out, however, that even the greatest novels are *nothing but* paper, ink, a certain amount of miscellaneous misinformation, and imagination.

The space age opening before our eyes — perhaps someone actually reading these words will go to the moon if not farther — is the end result, scientifically supported, worked out with infinite toil, of man's first mad, unreasonable image of himself flying. When it was first entertained, a good while before Daedalus, that image was about as adapted to reality as if I were to feel the urge to lie, like Ariel, in a cowslip's bell. Yet today we do fly. Science fiction once prophesied, in its apparently wild flights of fancy, many of the aerial feats that have in fact come to pass. Are these the only phantasies which are allowed to come to pass? May not what science fiction calls teleportation also come to pass, along with the contents of that bottle in *Alice in Wonderland* marked "Drink Me," and it be possible for, not me maybe, but some woman in the future to become tiny and find herself curled inside that golden cup?

The principle embodied here, I think, is that what man can imagine, he may one day achieve. We know the part that mathematics, physics, chemistry, mechanics play in such miracles. We know the role, on the plane of human character, that persistence, courage, dauntlessness, and what is sometimes called cussedness play. Yet I believe there is in addition another element in what makes possible the transformation of dreams into realities, in what turns man's stark-naked fancy into an entity irreproachably clothed: a fact. Perhaps we might look into how imagination works, to find what this element may be.

Even to the people who are on the imagination side of the dichotomy — writers who make a living, like the man in Daudet's story "The Golden Brain," by pulling out of their heads handfuls of something that passes for gold — there is something exasperating about imagination when it is improperly used. Recently a publisher sent me galleys of a first novel by a young woman of twenty-three — a girl for whom high hopes are entertained in literary circles. On its very first page the novel, which begins in the year 1929, speaks of lace on the voluminous petticoats of one character; a little further on, of a middle-aged lady who is wearing a black bonnet, and of someone else coming to New York to find a dressmaker to run up a few black silks for the conventional mourning she is going into. I *was* exasperated. People of the kind the author was writing about simply didn't do these things, or wear these things, in the place and time she was writing of. This is, for any reader, what the English call off-putting. Imagination, to be what it ought to be — and I mean by that to flower — should not only be directed in the proper way, but should be directed toward the proper things. When Max Perkins told me not to know too much about the Paris of the Nineties, he didn't mean not to know what is readily knowable about it. He didn't mean me, for instance, to dress my characters in the fashions of the Directoire.

Now when a man faces something knowable and real, whether it is an object, a dilemma, or a historical event, he directs toward it the battery of his functions of knowing — sensation, which tells him something is there; thought, which reasons what it can be; feeling, which tells him what it means to him; and intuition, which sporadically informs him of the why, the whence and the whither of the object. These four functions go to produce a total judgment, as far as the man is able to utilize them. It is when he is faced with the unknown that man's imagination springs to the fore, like a fountain gushing up out of a rock. It presents him not with information about the unknown as it really is, but with an image of what the unknown is like. Nobody, for instance, knows what imagination really is. But it is like, as I said, a fountain gushing up out of a rock.

In a sense, then, the workings of imagination can be said to be the facing of the unknown by the unknown. Man cannot endure not knowing about things; he can endure it even less than knowing about them, which is pretty unendurable too. So, out of ignorance, up springs fancy with its pictures. Sometimes, as we have seen, a lady's making her private image of what she doesn't know can lead her to put her finger in a fuse socket, with results we may mournfully deduce. Or imagination can make a breach between friends, founded on nothing more malign than a moment's brusqueness. Or imagination can lead to the creation of the flying machine. Or to *War and Peace* — the novel, as well as the states of affairs — for, as John Knowles says in his novel *A Separate Peace,* wars are made by something ignorant in the human heart. In any of these cases, original motive power was supplied not by altruism or knowledge, but by fancy, idle or employed.

Who makes images of the image-maker when the image-maker's busy making images? *We* might make, of the faculty of imagination itself in its relation to the real world, an image of the blind spot in the eye. There is a test, similar to one oculists use, which demonstrates the existence of this blind spot. Take a sheet of typewriter paper and draw a black spot in the middle of it. Three inches to the right of the spot, draw an X. Now cover your left eye with your hand, hold the paper at arm's length, and bring it slowly nearer your face as you keep your right eye fixed on the black spot. At some point the X will suddenly disappear completely. You can pin down the exact distance from your eye at which that X you drew might never have been put to paper. The cause for this hole in your field of vision is that the optic nerve, which connects the retina with the brain, is, itself, sightless. Therefore, opposite to where the nerve end empties into the eye is this tiny blind spot. Needless to say, your left eye has its blind spot too. Each eye compensates for the other's minuscule lack. It is rather a humbling test to take. It makes you realize you might be missing something, and there is, also, a flaw in yourself you hadn't suspected. As a matter of fact, some percentage of motor accidents is said to be caused by the blind spot when it isn't compensated for. At such times the other eye did not sufficiently hasten to explain that little unseen area in terms of what, in all reason, it had to be.

Not in this way, but in something like this way, imagination attempts to explain to man what he doesn't know, in terms of other things that he does know. *Like* is the key word. Like a poultice comes silence, writes Oliver Wendell Holmes — maybe because he was a doctor. Like an eagle caged I pine, writes Epes Sargent when he is feeling land-locked and forlorn ashore. Forlorn — the very word is like a bell. But Keats, a much better poet, seldom used the actual word "like." As Mr. MacLeish has pointed out, a poem should not mean but be. In other words, like the flying machine, the poem is an imagining that has completed itself; that has come true. In some way, while facing the unknown with the unknown, the mind of the imaginer has contrived to arrange before its spot of blindness a compensation which truly fits, which does not mean but turns out to be. Only one person makes this image of the hitherto unknown; but other people — society, if you like — read the poem, and in the case of a Keats, at any rate once he was dead, society accepts it as true. James Russell Lowell says, "The story of any one man's real experience finds its startling parallel in every one of us." Now, "universal" seems to me to be one of those words people use when they can't explain why a piece of writing should be so good. I'm not going to use it here. But how are we to explain the affinity between Keats and a host of prudent readers who are nothing like Salinger's dear John who would not put his scarf on? How is it that on some level Keats and his readers become, not the artist-versus-society, but the artist-and-society?

It isn't only in the arts that the unseeing is used to face the unseen and, by the use of images, discern truth. The Rorschach test is one example of imagination's supplying information, not about the object, but about the subject. Falling in love is a total expense of feeling which reveals much more about the lover than it does about the loved one. Another example is from the field of chemistry and is part of a long account written by the chemist August Kekulé of his coming upon his famous benzene theory. "I was sitting engaged in writing my textbook," he writes, "but it wasn't going very well. I turned my chair toward the fireplace and sank into a doze. . . . Atoms flitted before my eyes." (As they had before, when "I saw that frequently two smaller atoms were coupled together, that larger ones seized the two smaller ones, and that all whirled around in a bewildering dance.") "Smaller groups now kept modestly in the background. My mind's eye, sharpened by repeated visions of a similar sort, now distinguished larger structures, of varying forms. Long rows close together, all in movement, winding and turning like serpents! And see! What was that? One of the serpents seized its own tail and the form whirled mockingly before my eyes. I came awake like a flash of lightning. I spent the night working out the consequences of the hypothesis. . . . If we learn to dream, gentlemen, then we shall, perhaps, find truth. We must take care, however," the scientist adds, "not to publish our dreams before submitting them to proof by the waking mind. Countless germs of mental life fill the realm of space, but only in a few rare minds do they find soil for their development."

According to Beatrice M. Hinkle, in *The Recreating of the Individual*, the serpent with its tail in its mouth is a symbol of narcissism, the self-enclosed infantile state, and at the same time a symbol of the highest human development. The point to note is that what turned out to fill the missing need, the unseen area, in the benzene theory was not anything primarily pertinent to chemistry, but a particularly subjective image.

Again, Anatole France, in one of his stories about historical church figures, tells of the Abbé Oegger, who was a dreamer, much given to worrying, particularly about Judas. It worries the Abbé incessantly that Judas — so the teachings of the

Church declare — was condemned to eternal punishment. The Abbé feels that Judas was, actually, doing God's work; that his betrayal of Christ was essential in enabling Christ to complete his work of redemption of mankind. For if it hadn't been for Judas's act, Christ could not have been crucified; hence, not resurrected either. Therefore, Oegger feels, a merciful God could not possibly have damned Judas. But he is tortured by doubts. One night he went into the church and prayed to God to send him a sign. Thereupon he felt a heavenly touch on his shoulder. Next day he went to the archbishop and told him he had made up his mind to go out into the world to preach the gospel of God's infinite forgiveness toward sinners. Not long after going out into the world, France's story ends, Oegger left the Catholic Church and continued his preaching within the fold of Swedenborgianism.

C. G. Jung, in commenting on this account, points out an interesting angle to Oegger's obsession with the problem of Judas. "When he becomes a Swedenborgian, we can now understand his Judas phantasy," Jung writes. "Oegger was himself the Judas who betrayed his Lord. Therefore he had first to assure himself of God's mercy, in order to play the role of Judas undisturbed. For him, Judas was the symbol of his own unconscious intention; and he made use of the symbol in order to reflect upon his own situation — the direct realization would have been too painful for him." By the analogy we have been using, we might say that Oegger was using an outside unknown to solve the problem of an inside blind spot, since at the time of his absorption with Judas, Oegger was quite blind to the plan that was forming itself deep in him. His worries about the archtraitor of Christendom fitted his own unacceptable intention. There was a sort of likeness between part of him and Judas.

A while back I said I believed there to be another element in the transformation of dreams into realities, quite apart from scientific verification of hypotheses and the application of elbow grease. It is this third element which I have been attempting to demonstrate in the two examples just cited, in which the solutions to the problems involved were provided not by any conscious functioning, but by imagination itself. Not Kekulé's scientific knowledge — profound as that needed to be — but drowsy fancy supplied the missing link in the benzene theory. Not any reasoning of Oegger's about the morality of an intention he didn't even know he had enabled him to prepare the ground for his defection from Catholicism. Instead, a long period of worrying about the fate of Judas culminated in a conviction that mercy would be shown a defector.

That element in imagination which leads out of dreamland into the world of facts, actions, and reality is to be found, I believe, in its peculiar two-way functioning. Things that are unknown and terrible in the outside world are like known things in man's inner world. Conversely, unknown and terrible inner things can be compared to things that are visible abroad. The ocean, for example, in its violence, turbulence, immensity, calms — its grandeur — is like an element that exists within man's mind. On it, he often feels himself to be sailing; or from it, stepping ashore on some desert island. Or he is being shipwrecked on it, or stranded in a Sargasso Sea. It is easy to assume that the existence of this inner element, which can not only seem real but behave with such reality, can be traced to the centuries of man's watching, in fear and trembling, the behavior of the real ocean. However, this explanation will not entirely cover many cases, such as that of a friend of mine, a writer born and brought up in the Middle West, who used to hear when lying in bed at night going to sleep in Wisconsin a rhythmical roaring which he always thought of as the sound of the sea. It was not until he was twenty-two and had just arrived to be a graduate student at Harvard that he visited a friend on the North Shore of Massachusetts. They walked across the Ipswich marshes after supper, in the dusk, and as they grew nearer to the beach my friend began — *began once more* — to hear a roaring, for the first time in reality but entirely familiar to him in imagination: the ocean's sound.

Since man did, in a preliminary manifestation, crawl out of the ocean and is still composed largely of sea-water, it is at least conceivable to think of him as bearing the sea within him, as a conch shell does. It would be hard to say which, then, comes first for man when he imagines — the outside sea or the inside one. Likewise, it may readily be seen that one of these two oceans has to be an image of the other. One is the reality; the other is the symbol. But which is which? It is easy to say that the outside sea is the real one. But when a woman is so abnormally fearful of the ocean that she won't go on it even in fair weather with a light breeze, or if she looks into its green and wavering depths with horror and has no trust in a quite seaworthy vessel, isn't she making of the outside ocean an image of the kind of ocean she has inside her? The fact is that it is characteristic of imagination to move from the outer to the inner, and from the inner back to the outer, in a wavelike motion. In the world of the imagination correspondences exist to everything. My heart is like a singing bird. A drowsy numbness pains my sense, as though of hemlock I had drunk. My luve is like a red, red rose.

In the world of outer reality, of course, everything is unique. Each snowflake in a blizzard is a little different from every other snowflake. A poem created by comparing things to other things is, once out in the world, unique. As a completed poem, it should not mean but be. Gertrude Stein's rose, she insisted, was like nothing but itself. A jet plane — the end result of some poor wretch in antiquity looking up at the sky with the feeling that part of him was like a bird and could fly — is not really like a bird, after all. It is like nothing but a jet plane. Man still tends to feel there is something in him like a bird, but now he sees that it isn't a plane at all, because the feeling is still in him, quite unsatisfied by his ability to reach Paris in six and a half hours. One quality of the real world, in fact, would seem to be uniqueness. I think we can say that when a dream has been transformed into a reality, when a poem is successful, it is not like any other real thing. In the outside world it is only when a creation is unsuccessful, incomplete — as in the case of a derivative painting, or when a person is living somebody else's life — that things are like other things.

It is in the world of the imagination that things are incomplete, and identifiable only by being compared to other things. The comparison helps them to become complete and real. My luve, Burns says, is like a red, red rose. Does he mean a girl, when he says his love, or does he mean the love he has for the girl? Does he mean a rose in the garden, or the rose his heart feels like? What does it matter? He has the world with him. Everybody knows how a rose feels, and how a girl smells. Everybody knows how a feeling blooms, and how red sings. Rose, girl, love, red make up a completed line of poetry that is not like any other. Christina Rossetti's heart was not really a singing bird; it was like a singing bird. That was the nearest she could get on that try. Next time round she said it was like an apple tree; after that she tried a rainbow shell; and by the time she got through the reader had a very fair idea of what Christina Rossetti's heart felt like because her love had come to her, poor soul.

When I was writing this section about imagination, I thought of calling it "The Role of Society in the Writer." The reason I didn't was that I felt sure that somewhere along the line it would get misunderstood as what I don't want to talk about and am not talking about — the role of the writer in society. Society, if we think of it as an agglomeration of people standing for the social status quo, plays a very large part in the writer, particularly in the novelist. Frank O'Connor has defined the subject of a novel as almost invariably the relation of the individual to society. Since the novel is a work of the imagination, however, not only its characters are imaginary, but also the society to which they are set in relation. Sometimes the society in books is very imaginary indeed, like the various societies in *Gulliver's Travels,* or like the small, furry talking animals that constitute the good society in *The Wind in the Willows.* Sometimes it is less imaginary, like Thackeray's heartless society in *Vanity Fair,* or Dickens's sadistic society in *Bleak House.* Or like Jane Austen's decorous society; in her case it must be pointed out that a society set in the England of the early nineteenth century is imaginary indeed which never converses on the burning topic of the Napoleonic Wars. Jane Austen's notably talkative characters never even refer to them.

The real hero of Jane Austen's novels, is, as a matter of fact, society.

Times have changed. I can't imagine a novelist today who would make a hero out of society — although early nineteenth-century English society wasn't precisely utopian either. Jack Kerouac is one of the modern novelists whose images of the social status quo seem terrifying; like villainous. In *The Dharma Bums* there is a passage in which Rosie, who had once been "a real gone chick and friend of everyone of consequence," goes crazy and tries to cut her wrists. She insists there is going to be a big revolution of police. "The police are going to swoop down and arrest us all, and we're going to be questioned for weeks and maybe years, till they find out all the sins and crimes that have been committed. It's a network, it runs in every direction, finally they'll arrest everyone in North Beach and Greenwich Village and Paris, and then finally they'll have everybody in jail. They're going to destroy you. I can see it, it's only begun. Oh, the world will never be the same!" Although this is said by a disturbed character, her speech is given a vital importance in the novel, motivating the protagonist, Ray, to leave town and hit the road once more. "Isn't this the time to start following what I know to be true?" he asks himself; then: "I said goodbye to Japhy and the others and hopped my freight back down the Coast to L.A. Poor Rosie, she had been absolutely certain that the world was real, and fear was real; and now what was real?" Kerouac would seem to reveal, at its punitive, disciplinary worst, the Beat's image of our repressive society. It is also the view of those whom Joseph Margolis calls the latter-day knights: the delinquents. On the other hand, it is important to note that an equally modern and rebellious novelist, Paul Bowles, can rail at today's society in exactly opposite terms, seeing it as slack, inert, and overpermissive.

The reproachfulness I referred to earlier, of readers who discover that fictions they like are not true, is of course absolutely nothing to the reproachfulness of readers who suspect fictions they do not like *are* true. It took Asheville, North Carolina, a long time to recover from what it considered Thomas Wolfe had done to it. And when recently a movie was made, in the mining town in England where D. H. Lawrence grew up, of *Sons and Lovers*, it was found the townspeople had not even yet forgiven Lawrence for what they feel he did to it. A newspaper story about the movie quoted several oldest inhabitants, who said exactly what Asheville used to say — "We weren't a bit the way he said we were." I agree; I am sure that they were not. I am sure the town in Lawrence's novel is like no other on land or sea. Lawrence's novel is unique. A successful work of art is not *like* any other thing in the real world.

But just as God created man in his own image, man does create his works of art (or his anything else, his chemical formula or his plans to defect) in the image of himself. The two-way functioning of the imagination thus holds good for one further step. What the writer creates is like something in its creator. One reason a society can get so angry at novelists is because society, too, has done some imagining. It has imagined that by some feat of magic writers can look into the secret lives of people they take as models for their characters. This seems to many an infringement of privacy. But a case can be made for what I think is the fact: that no one really knows anything about anyone else except by deduction and induction, intuition and empathy. Certainly not by magic. The rest is all imagination. Since Sidney's long-gone day, "Look in thy heart, and write" has meant just that. It does not mean "Look in someone else's heart"; for that is impossible.

In the greatest novels — novels as different as *War and Peace* and *Howards End* — we do, however, see demonstrated something far more magical. This is the existence of a brotherhood of man, an underlying unity, demonstrated precisely because the universal recognitions that such novels awake are born not out of a shared experience but out of a solitary one. A man alone has made images that turn out to be common to all. His characters sprang not so much from observation as from imagination. That character in his novels which is society is much the same order of image as we all use when we imagine, fearfully, "What will people think?" or, longingly, "I wish I were like other people." But it should never be forgotten that in all his projections, the novelist is expressing not the self he knows himself to be but a self of which he is so far unaware. Any creation of the imagination, whether in art or elsewhere, could offer a unique opportunity to fulfill the Delphic injunction: Know thyself. A novel, like any other invention — a poem, a picture, a theorem in science — is potentially a discovery and an uncovering as much as it is a creation.

It is true that all of us, everybody, imagines society and the world outside us. Society is so amorphous you only *can* imagine it. But we have been taught to distrust our imagining of it, and to try to keep a check on our images by reason and experience. The writer, on the other hand, has learned to trust his imagination most of all. He does not merely imagine society, he makes society a character in his works, with which the other characters must struggle. Often, like Rosie, they are defeated by it. Sometimes they conquer, as Fielding and Aziz did in *A Passage to India*, when they came out on top of the English colony. The writer, all alone in his study, all alone in his head, can make endless images of society and set them up in a poem, a novel, a short story — forms which, as we have seen, become realities once they are completed and out in the world.

Just as it is hard for people who distrust imagination to accept the idea of living by the imagination, it is hard for the writer to accept that he is anything else but a writer. But statistically the writer is a member of society as well, whether he wants to be or not. There is no such thing as not being a member of society. He can be a reluctant member, if he chooses. He can be an irresponsible member, or a dissident member, or a useless member. But he is a member, a part of why society is whatever it is. There are writers of today rejecting, or unaware of, the member of society in themselves, to be seen on every hand railing at society, at war with it. George Barker, the British poet, has even advocated the complete cutting loose of the artist from society, to go it alone on standards set solely by himself. In my view this is alarming, not only because an artist cut off from real society would have nobody to communicate with except other artists, but because it means that the artist would be, all unconscious of what he was doing, splitting himself in two, the social side from the writer side, following the profound schismatic tendency that has appeared since Luther in every activity that goes deep into man's psyche. Who is going to heal him?

As we have seen, the society the writer puts into his work is

not real society. It is merely his image of society. It is like society. It is something, in the common phrase, out of his own
head. If he pictures society as hateful and vicious, he pictures something in himself, unrecognized; some Judas to his
Christ. Mr. Kerouac's police-state version of society, for instance, must needs compensate a conscious self much in want
of discipline. And indeed, is that not what we do find in the
undoubtedly gifted Kerouac? The writer often tends to feel
he is misunderstood. But the real question is, Just who is failing to understand him? The writer generally feels that when
he lives in his imagination, he is somehow unique. But we
have seen that actually it is only in the real world that things
are ever unique: complete poems, complete inventions, complete people. In the world of the imagination, a thing can only
be like something else. What the writer's self, apart from his
imagination, is like is the thing he writes.

Keats's beautiful and frightening "La Belle Dame Sans
Merci" expresses, as few poems have, a particular doom. It is
the fate of one who loiters on the inhuman, cold hill's side of
imagination after the granary is full and the harvest's done. If
only, armed by what he learned of his danger in the dream of
pale kings and princes, that knight could have fled a land
where no birds sing, back to workaday life! She who has him
in thrall — that faery's child — both reigns over poetry and is,
to get down to earth, almost a clinical picture of the deathly
radiant mother who draws her love-victims to her in the embrace of tuberculosis. To us with hindsight, it is unendurable
to realize what Keats knew about himself — and at the same
time didn't know. The wavelike motion which we have seen

imagination describing is actually itself an imitation of — it is like — the wavelike motion of real life. Real life flows in to the real self, and out to the real world again.

There was once a monk who, in order to escape the temptations of the world, the flesh, and the devil, went into the desert to live alone in a cave. But at night, in the shadows his solitary fire cast against the walls of his cave, he found himself haunted by the same voluptuous and carnal images he had run away from. Just so the writer, in order to write, is obliged to leave the world of society, at least for the hours in which he is writing. "Solitude," Lowell said, "is as needful for the imagination as society is for the character." The act of creation has been called one of the three most complete solitudes known to man's mind; the others being, I believe, sleep and prayer.

Thus sequestered, the writer's imagination is freed to pursue its work of endless likening, of visualizing the unknown in terms of the known. Only shadows of the real world, of society, haunt his study's walls. He can fight the shadows, he can scream at them, he can put out his fire and say there are no shadows. Or he can recollect himself. He can know the shadows for his social self, which is always there whether he likes it or not. So he begins to make his peace with the world and to build a bridge between imagination and reality.

In my opinion the artist and society are complementary to each other and cannot be divided except artificially. Even then the attempt is disastrous. What the imagination is in relation to is whatever is unknown and latent within the status quo. Imagination's special function is to bring to light this hidden X, through a process of comparing it to what is already visible. If it were possible to uncover the unknown by means other than imagination, it would no doubt have been done long ago.

Imagination's purpose is to express what is otherwise inexpressible — the stone that throbs, the ice that burns. Status quo and imagination cannot exist healthily apart. For the writer to reject society and the world — of whom all his images are made, for whose ears all his insights are intended — would be as tragic as when society denies, as it so often does, the imagination. Those who refuse to accept imagination into themselves, cutting it off in terms of *nothing but*, reject their own future. They restrict life to what has already, up to date, been realized.

Imagination is new reality in the process of being created. It represents the part of the existing order that can still grow.

❦

THREE

The Novel and the Short Story: Differences

WHEN, once upon a time, I was asked to speak on "Content in Fiction," I drifted into the kind of woolgathering that passes for wondering what somebody means by some phrase and is actually, I suspect, simply another device by which the unconscious keeps one from getting down to work. What, I said to myself, do they mean by content? What is content?

Actually, content does seem to be one of those words, of which area is another, contact still another. Skills is another, though I know what *skill* means. I don't know what con'tent means. I didn't think they could possibly have meant content'. Content' in fiction — at least in the writing of it — there just isn't any. Writing fiction, in fact, means lack of content'.

At a lecture of Auden's one spring in Oxford, I heard someone say of him, "I like the shape of his mind but not its contents." It brought to mind a picture, far from accurate, of Mr. Auden's head as a kind of exquisite Lowestoft bowl with nothing in it but some stale corn flakes. The word contents I seem to understand, all right, but not con'tent. Anyway, I went and looked up con'tent in the Oxford English Dictionary and definition number 1 said that that which is contained, as in a vessel, is now used only in the plural (or form I already understand). Definition number 2 is "tenor, purport." (The tenor, purport of fiction?) Number 3 is "the substance or matter of art as opposed to its form." (That is, of course, the corn flakes as opposed to the Lowestoft bowl.) Number 4 is: "containing power, as of a vessel; capacity; 1491." Number 5 is "extent, area (now rare), 1571; volume, now the usual sense, 1612."

About this time my conscience told me I really had to get to work, so I settled for "containing power, as of a vessel"; both because I like the idea of the vessel, and because I do think that fiction contains power. If, then, we are to think about fiction as a vessel, what is that vessel like?

Today the two main fictional forms are the novel and the short story. They are not only different in length, in capacity for getting a lot of words in; they are totally different in kind. They try to do different things. A novel is not an extended short story, and when somebody tries to extend a short story into a novel, he can successfully do so only by adding a number of new qualities. A short story is not a short novel — far from it. There is also the novella, or long short story, which comes in between and has qualities common to both. But for the purposes of making clear distinctions I want to speak only of the novel and the short story, in terms of what it is they are trying to do. Both, I should hasten to say first, are of course stories in the sense that Randall Jarrell uses (as we will see in a later section) when he says that a story is a wish, or a truth, or a wish modified by a truth; is in this sense a dream. Stories can be as short as a sentence, he adds, giving an example from Bion the Greek poet: "The boys throw stones at the frogs in sport, but the frogs do not die in sport but in earnest." Stories can also mean *Great Expectations* or *War and Peace*. Stories are, in fact, in everything. One of the most encouraging moments of any writer's life is that moment in which he realizes he never need fear for the lack of a story to tell. Stories are everywhere, and if the writer cannot find them, the trouble is in himself. I have sometimes thought one need only remember that all that is wanted to convert a real event or a real person into a story is to imagine what would have happened if what did happen hadn't; what a person would be like if his life were quite otherwise. When one is in the groove, stories are suddenly in everything one passes on the street, every face, every stone, every window glanced into. In fact, content in fiction is, I expect, just that: stories. Fiction contains all kinds of possible stories.

But once we have said this, we must go on to say that as far as the novel and the short story forms are concerned, it is as if we had been speaking of shipping in general, of the Merchant Marine, or of the U. S. Navy. What we are trying to discuss here is that dreadnaught the novel and that PT boat the short story. Like those vessels, they are designed for differing tasks. The short story, Frank O'Connor says, consists of "its attitude to Time. In any novel, the principal character is Time. Even in inferior novels, the chronological ordering of events establishes a rhythm, which is the rhythm of life itself. But what to the novelist is the most precious element in his work, is a nightmare to the short story writer. He is all the while trying to get round the necessity for describing events in sequence. . . . Every short story represents a struggle with Time — the novelist's Time — a refusal to allow it to establish its majestic rhythms. It attempts to reach some point of vantage, some glowing center of action, from which past and future will be equally visible. The crisis of the short story *is* the short story, and not, as in the novel, the logical, inescapeable flowering of events. The short story springs from the heart of a situation rather than mounts up to and explains it."

The short story does not deal, O'Connor goes on to say, "with types, or problems of moment."

The differences between the short story and the novel, he says, "suggest that the difference has something to do with the attitude that the two art forms impose on their writers. I have no doubt that the difference is in the attitude to society. The thing which makes an Irish novel impossible is that the subject of a novel is almost invariably the relation of the individual to society; and Ireland does not have a society which can absorb the individual. As a critic put it, 'Every good Irish novel ends on a ship to England or America.' But the emotion of Gabriel Conroy in *The Dead* is not conditioned by society, and the loneliness of the people in *Winesburg, Ohio* is not likely to be changed by any change in their social condition. Their troubles 'are from eternity and shall not fail.' In fact the short story, compared with the novel, is a lyric cry in the face of human destiny. The short story writer is not a soldier in the field, but a guerilla fighter, fighting the obscure duels of a great campaign. He stands always somewhere on the outskirts of society."

I think this is all true, and I think one can so expand the

images in what O'Connor says here as to relate them even more closely to life. The short story, while it can involve a number of personal destinies, or a number of events, does tie them all into a crisis. Now a crisis, in fiction, means a decision. Something is decided, a choice is made, a direction is taken. Thus I have always found it helps, in getting a feeling for what the short story may rightly attempt, to equate this crisis, or decision, with the life of the individual in relation to himself alone, since one's entire autonomous activity can be boiled down to the making of choices. In contrast, the novel may be thought of as a looking outward — more loosely, more diffusely; all decisions made. The novel as a form is analogous to the individual out in the world, whether just physically so or by virtue of being grown up. It is this encounter of people with each other in a society that sets up the novel's tension.

A short story can be like a real person, or a real problem, or a real emotion, but a novel is like life itself, only at one remove (which is always a relief, of course). When I say the novel deals with a number of personal crises set into relation with society, I don't mean anything elaborate or profound about society. I know there isn't any, etc., etc. . . . What I mean is the group of people within whose orbit the characters in the novel are operating. I mean hip society, or the society of Angry Young Men, or the bullfighting set, or any other established group of people one could specify. I believe this setting of the individual against society as in life, but at one remove, accomplishes something of which E. M. Forster says in *Aspects of the Novel*, "In the novel we can know people perfectly and apart from the general pleasure of reading; we can find here a compensation for their dimness in life." The attraction of the short story form is the attraction of the personal crisis; but the lure of the novel is the lure of great, big, disorderly, irritating, marvelous life itself.

Or I might compare the novel not to the short story world of a precision watch but to the great inchoate workings of an alternately benevolent and menacing juggernaut. The inner arrangements of that juggernaut are what go into the novel — are that content we started by mentioning. They are the power that the vessel — that is to say the form — contains. (I know that is not what the OED means by "containing power, as of a vessel," but it is what I mean.)

Obviously, then, ideas for a novel and ideas for a short story are of quite different orders. Not in length, again, not even in complication, necessarily, but in kind. When I get an idea for a story or a novel it is my habit to write it down on anything that happens to be around and then to put it in a box that originally was sent me from Miller & Rhoads in Richmond with some piqué collars in it. It seems to be the right size for the pieces of paper that I seem to find around to write on.

After a while I usually get another idea that is connected with the first idea and I paperclip it to the first idea. When there gets to be quite an accumulation, it seems to be about time to start writing the story or novel around which the notes have accrued.

I thought it might be a good idea if I took a few of the pieces of paper out of the box and used them here, to illustrate if possible the difference between a novel idea and a short story idea. Likeness between ideas for the two forms is soon disposed of. Ideas for novels and ideas for short stories have both got to have in them people, events, feeling, scenes, meaning. The *difference* in the nature of the forms is harder to define. Here, then, are a few ideas off the top of my box.

"Story about Mary M. She has lost her religious sense and derides it all as irrational, having revolted against a convent girlhood. She sees no meanings in anything, as in *Doctor Zhivago*. She said it was pointless. She thinks of everything in terms of her own death, and plans her house and garden in terms of how long she will live — i.e., will the bush, or slip-cover material, last out her lifetime. She is beginning to lose her sense of the value of style — can't bother to be chic, and chic was her great talent. She is sweet, kind, harmless, adjusted to the community."

This is, of course, short story material; not only because it concerns the destiny of an individual in relation to herself, but because the spotlight is focused on one life, and because the story will have to be told in terms of one crisis, which crisis will have to tie up into a gestalt the elements of Mary M's choice against life and for death; her outer adjustment and inner defeat. I would say the story would have to hinge on that very giving up of the worldly talent for chic, since it is often to a character's most worldly values that his strength of soul is hitched. The reader would need to be able to see how in, say, not buying a pair of extravagant evening slippers because her rationalism told her she had no need for them, Mary was denying herself not so much the slippers as the last little ray of desire that reached out from her to them, leaving her in a sad marsh of adjustment to reality where her only yardstick of value is to be whether an object will last her lifetime.

Fitting an idea into a form is, possibly, comparable to the adjustment of the cargo into that ship, or vessel. Every writer has his own notions about how ideas are best made to fit the forms he attempts. My own notion is that the most important things to remember in writing fiction (of any kind) are: beginnings; the balance of forces, or tension; writing in scenes as far as is mortally possible; the motivations for action; and the making of skillful, unnoticeable transitions. In later sections these will be discussed in detail. Other writers will lay the stress on, say, dialogue, narrative, and characterization, but to my mind if one writes in scenes — living the scenes in one's mind, seeing the faces, hearing the voices — one will have achieved effective dialogue and characterization as well as avoided the nastiest pitfall of narrative — the telling-instead-of-showing, against which every teacher of creative writing inveighs.

If one subjects oneself to the discipline of these technical forces for communicating ideas to a reader, the chances are greater that one will gain the effect that all novelists are struggling for: the effect of life. The effect of life has little to do with real life. Being an effect, it is a part of art, of that prestidigitation of which William Maxwell says, "What is achieved by these writers? Not life, of course, not the real thing; not children and roses; only a facsimile that is called literature. To achieve this facsimile the writer has more or less to renounce his birthright to reality. Why, then, should the successful manipulations of illusions be everything to a writer? Why does he bother to make up stories and novels? You might as well ask a sailor why it is that he has chosen to spend his life at sea."

We might examine the story idea I took off the top of my box to see what would have to be done with it to make it into not merely an idea for a story but a story, using those categories of technique which I believe in.

I think the tension the idea rests on, the balance of its forces, is that between life and death, the tension that has arisen because Mary M. has denied the values in her childhood religious training. She has chosen to live by reason, not realizing what she has done to herself thereby. She hasn't done anything to hurt the Church, after all; she has hurt only herself by denying validity to something which, if it is anything at all, is *for* the principle of life and *against* the principle of death.

All this would need to be understood by the author, then forgotten; and this seems as good a time as any to warn against the dangers of didacticism in fiction. It is terribly tempting to tell the reader what you mean — to explain that great truth that is yours to impart. Furthermore, if you don't tell the reader your truth, he might miss it, temptation goes on saying. Temptation should be resisted. A writer who is didactic must enjoy being so by himself, for he will very probably have no readers. Salinger is the only successful didactic short story writer I know of today. He merely proves the rule.

However, privately we may, as the corporate author of this story about Mary, realize that there *is* a balance of forces, a conflict, underlying it. Realizing that, we can go on to construct a story around some one moment when some choice of Mary's determines the remainder of her life. Let us imagine we have set the scene in a shop in the small town where Mary lives so well-adjustedly. The principal moment is going to be when she is drawn to some enchanting emerald satin slippers and decides against them. In deciding against them she will be deciding against life. But you can't tell this. You must show it, so Mary had better have a woman friend with her, because

I doubt that she is the type to be pally with the salesgirl. All that we know about Mary — about her Catholic girlhood, her method of selecting objects by the yardstick of whether they will last out her lifetime, her absorption with the idea of death, her refusal to see deeply into things (as in her saying *Dr. Zhivago* was pointless) — all these things will have to be shown or overheard, not told.

Again the principle of balancing forces arises, for we cannot have Mary solemnly telling a friend all the things that are wrong with her. Mary, of course, would believe in the complete rightness of her point of view; of pooh-poohing the irrational; of so-called common sense. Her dialogue will need to be self-assured, confident of acceptance from her companion, who of course lives in the small town to which Mary is so well adjusted.

But *is* it the town's approval which has made Mary so eager to turn against her own past? I don't think so. I think that something the reader must glimpse behind the scenes is Mary's husband, like a dark shadow. She loves him, and like so many, many wives, she takes his standards for her own. He is rationalistic, so she is too. He laughs at what he calls superstition, so she does too. Perhaps his opinions fit *him* snugly, like a comfortable shell, but the reader must see, though Mary cannot see, that they do not fit her.

The self-annihilation in which Mary is unconsciously engaged is motivated by a love for her husband which carries on where her convent training left off. Her husband's principles have merely been substituted for her earlier ones. Perhaps the real tragedy of Mary M.'s life is that in this choice that we will see her make she is like a little girl doing what she believes is right — as she was, after all, brought up to do. Only actually it is not what *she*, it is really what her husband, thinks is right. In rejecting the slippers she wants and doesn't need, she rejects her last silly, irrational, really alive impulse.

This is all awfully gloomy. This is the kind of small-town, earnest, would-be tragic plot people groan to read. But does it have to be? No, because the principle of the balance of forces tells us that the grimmest of tales have been told by skillful writers through the device of making them something else as well — frightening, violent, ridiculous. I think myself that Mary M.'s story is one that might be told ironically. One great value of irony is that it always makes the reader who gets the irony feel conspiratorial with the author. I think Mary M.'s dialogue might be, as we earlier suggested, bright, confident, full of small-town positiveness, unaware of that dark shadow the reader can see behind her own sensible, matter-of-fact presence.

The balance would then be between common-sense brightness and a realism which the reader would recognize as unreal, and the superstitiousness, the so-called irrationalism, which the reader would see as being the real truth and reality for Mary M. The spectacle of Mary M. taking her life apart into bits and flushing it away would be alleviated by the brisk finality with which she does it. The conflict implicit in the story would be that of doing the destructive thing under the conviction that it is the constructive one.

The slip of paper lying in my box under the one about Mary M. says, "The doctor told Annie's father" — Annie is my cleaning-woman in Virginia — "that he had six months to live. When the neighbors asked him if he had resigned himself, he said, 'Dr. Jesus ain't said nothin' to me yet 'bout dyin'. I ain't dyin'.' And he lived for 15 years."

That is in a sense a story, but not a "short story." The next slip of paper says, "Novel about Dorothy R. and what in the world Henry really was, under all that."

Why is this a novel idea, not a short story one? The reference was to a couple I once knew, and to the fact that the wife was one of those people who make their lives a success by what I guess one would have to call the power of positive thinking. She lived in a rather average house which to her was the most beautiful house in her city. Her husband was the most brilliant chemist the firm he worked for had ever employed. Her friends were unique. Her cleaning-woman was a jewel. But, especially, her marriage itself was the most romantic, the most rewarding, the most successful, ever consummated.

Perhaps only that stinker a writer could have found anything wrong with all this, and in real life I *didn't* find anything wrong with it. I was happy to be one of the real-life Dorothy's fabulous friends. What caught my interest and made me write down that note was sheer phantasy: What, I could not help wondering, was the husband, Henry, actually like? One didn't really get a chance to know, the build-up was such. He didn't seem like such a terrific charmer to me.

I hope it is clear that this idea has to be for a novel because it depends not only upon an individual's relation to himself but upon a number of other relationships — between a married couple, between friends; and most of all it depends upon the relationship between this couple and the society in which they live. Going about making a novel of it, using the same fictional tools that I listed in discussing the short story, would involve setting up a picture of the façade that society saw — the allegedly perfect marriage of Dorothy and Henry R.

Into conflict with this façade would at once come some doubt of its perfection, perhaps in the mind of a narrator. Another way to inject doubt would be to tell the novel through Dorothy R. herself, into whose own head has come the shadow of a doubt that all this she has built up into the pattern of perfection is not that at all. Something must have happened (crisis number 1) which has made her see, beyond possibility of quick mending, that Henry is, perhaps, dishonest, or unfaithful, or treacherous. Perfection versus imperfection is the balance of forces in this idea for a novel, and it is obvious that any resolution of it is going to lie in some combination of the imperfection implicit in perfection or, conversely, the perfection that there is in imperfection; or else in a refusal to resolve them at all. So much for the didactic framework which the writer cannot mention, must only know himself.

It seemed to me when I first had this idea that anybody with such a passion for making her life the epitome of the ideal must be eaten up by some fear of having it otherwise. Why must a normal, uneven life, a life with things the matter with it, be so unacceptable? The novel would be about what kind of past motivated Dorothy, as well as what Henry turned out really to be like.

It is a novel because to find out what Henry was really like, it would probably be necessary to explore an area larger than that the short story occupies. But I suppose one could turn this idea into another version of it that *would* make a short story. One could contrive an episode in which it is brought home to such a woman as Dorothy was, what all the time, under all her positive thinking, her husband was really like. Or it could similarly be brought home to a friend of theirs.

But what I saw was the relation of the R.s to their society. Dorothy's own relation to society is such that it seems necessary to her to have a perfect husband as well as a perfect everything else. The R.s' joint relation to the society in which they live, which would be interesting to invent, has become that of the perfectly matched couple to a rather less perfect environment. The working-out of the story, as story, would in some way have to alter that relationship, either by altering the attitude of one or the other R. to their society or by bringing some collective attitude of society's, perhaps hostility or suspicion, to bear upon the R.s.

Moreover, society in a novel is an actor quite as much as is that figure of Time O'Connor speaks of. In most novels society plays a part sufficiently active to allow it to be thought of as a character in the novel. That is to say, if we withdrew that character which society represents, the novel would fall apart. It is impossible to visualize *War and Peace* without the social worlds within which it moves, and which actively intervene to determine the action. In Jane Austen's novels society is all the time *there*, and all action would cease were it taken away. However, the short stories of Katherine Mansfield exist in the sunny or sinister flowerbeds of their characters' private lives. O'Connor's short stories are not about society in Ireland, but about Irish people. As he exclaims at the end of that article on short story writing which I have quoted, "It's a lonely, personal art."

Balance of forces, writing in scenes, strong and valid motivations are all required in the turning of an idea for any fiction, short or long, into its destined form. Transitions, on the other hand, are different in intention and in requirements in the novel from what they are in short stories. Transitions are, I think, together with beginnings, of all these tools for writing fiction the least often mastered, the most often overlooked. As far as transitions in the novel go, an excellent one in *A Passage to India,* where Dr. Aziz moves from Hamidullah's house up to Major Callendar's and so to the mosque where the momentous meeting with Mrs. Moore is to take place, takes four pages to accomplish.

A transition comparable in skill, within the short story, might take a sentence; two perhaps. The reason for this difference is in the matter of Time again. In the short story, as O'Connor pointed out, the writer is always striving for an effect of making it seem to happen within the boundaries of the crisis. The novel, on the contrary, progresses; as life does. It is essential that the reader get the feeling of life as it is being lived within this particular novel. In the case of *A Passage to India* the reader must feel several tempos: those of Moslem life, British life in India, the tempo of life among women together, that of men together, the quality life takes on in the juxtaposition of race with race, etc. All of this takes time. You cannot hurry the novel. That is why novel transitions must take so long. What they must accomplish is, as in the short story, the bridging of scene with scene, but in the short story the effort is toward making it all appear like *one* scene. The novel is told by a series of scenes, and what connects the scenes is the transitional passages.

In *A Passage to India,* one has been moved somehow from Hamidullah's to the mosque, but how this was accomplished one can hardly say, because all the while one was being fed more story. In a novel it is fatal for the transition passage not to do many other things besides be a transition passage. It must for one thing, without ever losing the tempo of the book as a whole, keep steadily supplying more and more clues to the secret of the novel, telling more and more fascinating things about its people, establishing the setting, perhaps. The transition passage, even while it is being a bridge between scenes, keeps steadily on with its showing-not-telling. Although it does not present a scene, it, too, can reveal, disclose. It does not — if it is a first-class transition passage — narrate, or very seldom.

In this passage of transition in *A Passage to India,* while Aziz is being got from Hamidullah's to the mosque, via Major Callendar's house, we learn dozens of things about him. That he is imprudent, that he is terrified (and with justification) of being snubbed by the British, because, as we see, British ladies are capable of behaving like no ladies with such as he; what his relations with the native servants of the British are like; the nature of his physique, the nature of India's soil, what a man like Aziz wears in the evening; what the mosque looked like from the outside; and many other details like so many bricks, building up the structure that is Forster's novel.

The transition passage in the novel of today seems to me to take the place of what used to be called the descriptive passages (the parts one skipped). I can't see any need for the descriptive passage as such. All that cannot be put into the mouths of characters can be pressed into service as material for the transition passage. Here is where to do any admiring of the scenery; not descriptively, informatively. Merely to describe seems to me to kiss with death. It is possible to think of the novel as one great body of water, a lake perhaps. The crests of its waves are the scenes, in which characters speak, move, reveal, act; the troughs of the waves connecting them are the transition passages — also revealing, explaining, disclosing, informing, all the while that they are stealthily — unnoticed by all but the unusually suspicious — moving the reader on and up to the crest of the succeeding wave.

The novel about Dorothy R. and her husband would have to be told by a series of scenes, connected by transition passages that prepared for, and referred back to, the scenes. The characters would keep breaking out, like foam, in their talking and acting; the transitions would keep flowing on, in a sense as though they had never been interrupted, as though they constituted the deep green water that underlies the whole. This wavelike motion of scene alternating with transition gives, I believe, that feeling of passage of time, of sense of life, which a novel requires. Put in a negative way, it is to say that a series of scenes in a novel which are connected by passages that the reader *realizes* are designed to connect them always seem jerky; they are not effective; they give no sense of time.

Of the first novels that are sent to me to read, I would say the thing most often the matter with them is that they have not achieved the sense of flow. This flow is the rhythm of life when translated into a novel through the art of fiction. Instead, they are full of stops and starts. With the novel it is essential, as indeed it is with all fiction, for the writer to think of the piece of work he is writing as a whole. The reason I cannot here work out fully the novel about Dorothy and Henry R., at least as much as I did the short story about Mary M., is that a novel is like a locomotive engine out in the untraveled desert which is laying down its own tracks for itself as it moves along. One cannot tell how a novel is going to develop or to end until one is inside it (and then it will probably be found on revision that one was wrong; that the characters want it some other way). But this is not quite what I mean by thinking of a novel as a whole. What I do mean is getting a feeling for the form, by reading enough novels. One gets a timing sense. One learns that each one of the scenes will be subservient to some larger whole. One finds that each transition passage serves the purpose of moving the novel on another step, within some larger framework. In writing the separate parts, a projected larger shape one does not really quite know the nature of is not lost sight of, but the novel is allowed to develop along lines it lays down for itself. At the same time one keeps a finger on its pulse, which will tell when it is time for the curve of the novel to come around and join on to itself.

I myself find it useful to draw a kind of picture, or diagram, of the shape of a novel I am engaged in. I don't know how it is going to end, I don't know how the characters are going to turn out, but I do know the shape of the novel — like a pair of mountain peaks, perhaps, with a deep valley between them; or like a diamond-shaped lozenge with a round hole in the middle — which serves as a guide to the relative height and intensity of the scenes I am writing. I should add that very often, on revision, I find that the shape as I had seen it was mistaken. It is not really diamond-shaped at all, this novel; it is circular. This is another thing about the novel; the writer can learn what it is like only by doing it, and he cannot hope to do it without making mistakes. I think the most important thing for him is to keep his mind open about the totality of his novel, so that he will never have a passage he is too fond of to take out if it strikes a wrong note; so that he will never hesitate to expunge a beginning that has come to seem out of balance with the end.

My father used to say that the secret of good writing is to go back over what you have done and cut out everything you like best. I don't quite agree, but I do feel that, especially with the novel, which takes so long to write, the writer must always keep the total novel as his true object; its good should be his aim, not his pet parts of it. He must not commit himself to any one fixed passage or person in it any sooner than he has to. He must keep the novel in his mind as a whole — fluid — as long as he possibly can, his imagination always free, never closed: to go on inventing, changing, reversing, disorganizing, re-creating.

The con'tent of fiction is, of course, stories; and what stories are are phantasies within a form or conscious design into which they may be sensed to fit. In all fiction, the degree of success achieved is determined by the strength of the phantasy world that supplies the action. To make a story follow the way something really happened in real life is to make everything as hard as possible for oneself. A wise writer tells about a life which is born, unfolds, flowers, changes, surprises, all within his imagination; he makes his characters like people he has known, but as they come to seem, with time, within his imagination. He will let his novel take whatever shape it takes for itself in his imagination. Then, perhaps, he will achieve an effect of reality.

The next note out of my box reads, "The young painter jeering at representational painters. He is an abstract expressionist. You see how he himself is bound to feel inferior when *he* becomes an older painter, whether young painters by that time really jeer at him or not." Is this a novel idea, or one for a short story?

The next note reads: "Alice P. Everyone spares her from realizing how useless she has in fact become as a result of drinking. If someone told her that she is a drunk and a parasite, what would happen?" What is this? Next note: "Two brilliant, very shy women, at swords' point with each other in a small dull town. They have nothing in common with anybody else, but toward each other they are filled with anger and antagonism." Why? What form does that take? Next: "A sympathetic sort of man like John, who has been active in the NAACP in NY, moves to the South. You see him groping around to find himself, by fitting into the upper-class pattern down here; and you see that is the *same thing* he was doing before, having no real convictions. Up there he was only seeking the wealthy, liberal society." What is that?

{ *FOUR* }

❦

The Novel: Character

I DON'T think there can be any question but what characters, characters that seem to live, are the most important single element in the novel. No one remembers novels for their style, or for the skill with which their plots were constructed. What we remember is Princess Marya and Prince Andrei; Becky Sharp and Lady Dedlock; Zuleika Dobson and Lewis Eliot's neurotic wife Sheila. Characters, characters that have a universal appeal, are, in fact, the life of a novel or a short story.

If it were possible to hand a young writer the secret for creating universal characters, or even humor characters, he would have it certainly within his grasp to write novels with appeal, however unfortunate they might be in other respects. Life is what gives a work of art power, or, rather, verisimilitude to life is. Of course such a present cannot be made, but there are some things which I feel do stand in a writer's way to impede him when he tries to construct characters which will live in his readers' minds and memories. I think I can begin by saying that life in the novel is the result of the writer's own exposure to real life. The two are not the same thing at all, but you cannot create life if you have never experienced any. Everything in the creation of a novel, it seems to me, is done within the head, cerebrally, except this one thing — the creation of character; and that is too, in part. But the reason why an overintellectual novel does not live, as Tolstoi does live, as Dickens lives, is, I think, that its creation took place too entirely within its author's rational, intellectual faculty. There must be feeling in it to make a character come to life; and feeling reaches, by its very nature, out, not in. I admired very much the novels of Mary McCarthy and that novel of Lionel Trilling's called *The Middle of the Journey* when I read them, but I find I cannot remember them today. They were admirable, but they did not live for me. Their characters were not alive.

One often hears the praises of careful research sung as an answer to the problem of verisimilitude. This works for some things, for background, for atmosphere even; not for character. Character has to have been felt — preferably on the quick, preferably with the author in a flayed condition. I once heard a best-selling novelist lecture on the importance of research to the creation of his characters. I went home and began to read the latest of this writer's novels. Early in it a character who is supposed to be a gentleman of the old school says "Pardon me." Now, a gentleman of the old school doesn't *say* "Pardon me." He says "Excuse me." As Maxwell Perkins of Scribner's used to say, "He didn't get it right." Research is not enough, without ear, and "ear" is one instrument of feeling.

There are of course two sources for characters in fiction — outside observation and the various aspects of oneself. In either case the process of the creation of a character in fiction is almost wholly subjective, so that these two sources for ideas for characters inevitably become merged. It is easy to demonstrate that a so-called objective novelist like Marquand was really writing about aspects of himself — as easy as it is to point to the undoubtedly universal nature of the subjective characters Kafka created. In either case, elements of both real, outer life and inner, private life are put into the smeltery of the creative process, where, as so many writers express it, they cook, before emerging as a new thing, a character. When the sources for character have been primarily outside, there arises that old, vexed problem of people outside thinking that they have been, to use their phrase, "put" in a book. A lot of this is of course rubbish. I once wrote a short story called "That Woman," just before moving to a town where I had never lived before. I was at once accused of having "put" a local lady named Vera, whom I had never met, in my story. This kind of thing proceeds from the misunderstanding of the writing process that exists in the mind of the non-writing public. When a non-creative person tries to write a story and fails to write a good one, his agonized insistence upon how like to real events the events in it were displays the nature of this misunderstanding. The average non-writing person, I think, imagines that in writing a story the author, by intention, focuses upon a real person, just as people in small towns focus when they gossip. Now there is nothing the matter with the instinct to gossip. Robert Frost puts gossip among his three greatest things in human thought. He defines it as "our guessing at each other, in journalism, novels, poetry. Gossip exalts, in poetry." The fact is, of course, that we are each totally alone and can only imagine things about each other, based on the little we know of ourselves. In fiction we have constructed a repository for this kind of gossip, which is based upon the imagination, not upon fact. You might say that in general the nearer a work of fiction comes to exact fact, the farther it is away from artistic truth. I was once highly complimented to get a fan letter about a story of mine, told in the first person, which had the narrator ending up, sad and frustrated, in Arizona. The letter said the story had moved its sender deeply, and added, "If I ever get to Arizona I shall try to find you and comfort you." I happen to live in Virginia, and I'm happy.

Thomas Wolfe is the classic example of the compulsive writer who creates character "first crack out of the box," the exposure to the cooking process of assimilation being hardly more than that given to a baked Alaska. The outraged reception Asheville first gave *Look Homeward, Angel,* before it learned to like being written about, does not, I think, signify, since it was so naïve as to represent more Hurt-Feelings Department than real or lasting wounds. The same cannot be said of the effect Wolfe's writing had upon people who were neither naïve nor provincial, to whom he dealt real and deep wounds. As a result of Wolfe's hewing so close to fact, Aline Bernstein came close to committing suicide, and did in fact suffer a severe nervous breakdown. In Elizabeth Nowell's biography of Wolfe she quotes Maxwell Perkins as saying to her, when Wolfe was contemplating the novel about Scribner's which did later appear after his death, "If Tom writes those things up and publishes them, it'll ruin those people's lives, and it'll be my fault" (because Perkins had given Tom some of the information). "If that happens," he went on, "I'll hand in my resignation and go live in the country." When Wolfe heard of this reaction, the nearest to compassion he displayed was to say that Perkins was playing the martyr. He was outraged. "I'm going to write as I please, and what I please, and nobody is going to stop me," he said. It was an admirable display of artistic integrity, but one may at this distance in time ask oneself, and stay some time for an answer: Who was of greater value to the entire world of letters — Wolfe or Perkins? Wolfe's self-absorption to the exclusion of anyone else's interests was, like compulsiveness itself, characteristic of the child. Elizabeth Nowell in fact quotes Sherwood Anderson as saying of Wolfe, "He is like his writing — generous and big in every day, but a good deal the great child."

Now I have nothing against children. I like children. All writers, all artists, have something of the child in them. What I am against is when the child in the artist (who, like real children, can be quite as destructive as creative) turns not only against its benefactors but at the same time against the adult it inhabits. Wolfe was destructive toward no one more than he was toward himself, when in the grip of his fearful drive. Without dragging in psychiatric definitions, I will merely sum up compulsiveness as the childish insistence upon gratification of a wish or impulse now; this minute; without further reflection; in just this original way and in no other; first crack out of the box. This trend is almost always seen in young writers, as well as in those unconscious artists of whatever age who are in love with their first impulse and will hear no criticism whatever of it, giving it a value which is overwhelming. Wolfe was such a writer. He says, "The business of the artist hurting people is for the most part nonsense. No one was ever hurt by a great book, or if he was, the hurt was paltry and temporary in comparison with the immense good that was conferred." That much is true. I agree. But I think Wolfe died before he got to be that great. I think he did hurt Aline Bernstein, Perkins, and others; and I think there are two kinds of creation of character, just as there are two kinds of gossip — the kind that hurts and the kind that does not hurt. One is forced to question whether a mind that could not even realize the hurts it was dealing Perkins had anything of the first value to say about life, at least at that stage.

However, compulsiveness hurts the wounder more than the wounded. Wolfe hurt himself most. All he is quoted as saying in the biography about art sounds fine; splendid; truer than true. All he is quoted as saying about living sounds undisciplined to the point of madness — and, indeed, it is interesting to note that Wolfe continually felt himself threatened by destruction in the forms of madness and of death — a death which did in fact untimely overtake him.

Compulsiveness in writing often attacks, in particular, a writer's ideas for his work. I have noted in many young writers' work the tendency to give the original idea for the story overwhelming value. The story has to be about the original concept, it has to be worked out as it first struck its author's mind, it has to end in just such a way. No room is left for possible improvement or maturing by mulling over. Those compulsive writers who say they cannot rewrite have the same feeling. I used to be one of them, but I can say from experience that when you find you are no longer bound to get the story right on the very first try, when you find that you can later change and correct and even entirely reconceive a story, the feeling is *not* one of being enslaved by technique or by self-criticism, the feeling is of being free. Free to do it better, free to get it closer to the heart's desire, free to keep trying until you get it right, free to throw it away.

What I have just said of compulsiveness in idea is true of character-building also. Wolfe produced the characters in his work, who were indeed of gigantic stature, first crack out of the box. In fact, by his own admission he strove most of all to make the life in his work not merely like, but almost identical to, outside reality. One of his greatest qualities — and there is no doubt that he had genius — was indeed for getting things right; the way they are: smells, sounds, sights of things. But he seemed uninterested in the idea of creating characters that belonged to him, not to reality. Or rather, he seemed to believe that through seeing characters he had known in reality through his own mind, he had sufficiently transformed them to call them his. But to their originals, Esther Jack did not seem very much transformed from Aline Bernstein, or Foxhall Edwards from Maxwell Perkins, nor did the characters that were drawn from Charles Scribner or Mrs. Wolfe or Mabel Wheaton. These characters, even in this raw state, did achieve a degree of greatness; the question is whether, if Wolfe had been able to make them his own, they would not have been much greater. I think they would. I think that if he had been able to make his characters uniquely his own, and universal as well, he would have been a greater artist than he was, at the same time becoming a far greater person.

Wolfe, however, rejected any attempt to bridle his characterizations, in the most violent terms. He felt that the slightest modification of his original vision would compromise his artistic integrity. He said, "When any man tries to exert this kind of control . . . to *modify* my material . . . because of some personal, social apprehension, he does the unpardonable thing. He tries to take from the artist his personal property, to steal his substance, to defraud him of his treasure, the only treasure he has. I am not going to be interfered with on this score. I get my material from my own living. And when any outer agency tries to interpose itself between me and any part of my own property, someone is going to get hurt." The outer agency of whom he was speaking was Perkins, whose help he had in fact sought in bringing order out of the chaos of his writing.

Now, it is true that the artist's integrity, his wholeness, must remain inviolable, untouched by outer interference. But what Wolfe first *sought* from Perkins was order, discipline; it was only later that he came to think of it as interference. He had grown up, emotionally, from the boy who had sought a father to a youth who wanted to stand on his own. His conflict, like the conflict of all artists, had become that between the integrity of the artist and the integrity of the human being. The artist must be true to art. The human being must be true to humanity. Neither of these two integrities can be sacrificed, without tragic damage or a fatal split. Somehow the two imperatives must be synthesized.

Whatever gestalt in the end resolves this conflict is, of course, the special experience of the individual writer. But there is this to be said: either the artist must serve the human being or the human being must serve the artist; or each the other. Goethe, who suffered greatly from the divided claims of his strongly marked emotional nature, said of himself that he would gladly sacrifice his art if by doing so he could become a greater man.

What Wolfe shouldn't have done was to betray confidences

that had been given to him as a person. I don't think anyone, artist or not, has the right to betray confidences. What Perkins had told him and what Mrs. Bernstein had given him were not what he called "material from my own living"; it was material from *their* living. He had no right to it, and in possessing himself of it I feel he came perilously close to betraying himself as an artist too, since kissing and telling is closer to the gossip column than it is to art. Wolfe's characters were journalism of the highest order — profiles, not creations; and the reason for this is that his compulsiveness, his being in such a tearing hurry, gave no time for his characters to gestate, to cook. He didn't trust himself to wait.

If his was compulsive character-building, what is non-compulsive character-creating? In the first place, it implies having confidence in one's creative powers. Many young writers write in such a tearing hurry because they fear if they don't, their talent will vanish and they will wake up to find they are insurance salesmen instead of writers. My father, who taught drawing and painting, used to say of students who feared that learning technique would injure their spark of genius, "Then it couldn't have been much of a spark of genius." The fact is that a fictional character can seldom be brought out into the round, made to live, except by trusting to a slow process of what may be called accruing. What is accruing?

With plots, accruing is what happens after a writer has had an idea for a story. He should make a note of it, to pin it down, and then forget it. It will come up to consciousness again, in a day or two or an hour or two, with additional facets — another scene, another idea, a new character. He should keep this up until he has enough to start writing with. Sometimes I have carried an idea for a story around with me for two or three years; I almost start to write it, and then a whole new facet gets added to it, somewhere out of consciousness, and it becomes a different sort of story.

So with characters. The secret of turning a character from journalistic reportage into a created image is, I think, to hang on to it. Don't write it down yet; hang on. The technique of creating characters that have had the unbilical cord to reality cut, thus releasing them to universality, is to let them grow within your mind.

The process really is much like the human process of gossip among people. A friend of mine in Washington went to Paris last winter. By the time she got back, the gossips had it that she had sold her house in the District, was never coming back, had cut all her hair off, had bought one hundred hats, and a few other tasty items no one of which happened to be true. The gossips were being, in their rudimentary and vestigial way, creators of accrued fiction.

I once started out with a character who was supposed to be a stinker in the novel he was in — the Southerner Boogher, in *Dear Beast*. He started from an idea of what I imagined the English husband of the anonymous author of *Madame Solario* to be; I had never seen him, but I had feelings about a man who would not let his wife publish a novel under her name. After a while I began seeing Boogher in the physical form of another man whom I really do know. This man is repulsive physically — thin and vulpine. I hoped the character would not have to look too much like the man I really knew, but suddenly Boogher acquired red hair overnight. The following week something curious happened, that has happened to characters of mine before. I began seeing Boogher in terms of the worst enemy of that vulpine friend of mine — a man whom he particularly detests. By this time the accrued character had got miles away from my vulpine friend, who has never seemed to see himself in the novel. I was much pleased when a Southerner said to me about the character of Boogher, in *Dear Beast,* "When I first read the book I thought, No one could be so awful as that. Then I realized I had a whole lot of kin were the spit and image of Boogher."

To gossip to oneself is just what it *is* legitimate to do about characters. Live in their lives. Move into their skins, have wish-fulfillment phantasies from where they stand. Free your mind from that first image of the real person who may have given you the idea for your character, and embroider; drift; hang on. Go back to your original source for the character again. Circle around the accrued image you are building, seeing him or her from a dozen different angles. Don't pin her down any sooner than you have to. Let your invention range. Give her one hundred hats.

Paucity of invention seems to be one of the things young writers say they feel oftenest troubled with. At one writers' conference I was given a number of short stories to read, all of which ended on a note of melancholy. I suggested that their authors try to write four alternate endings for them, and only then decide which was the proper one for their story.

In the same sense I think it is good to free oneself from the early commitment to one view of any character in one's work. In the case of Boogher, stinking as he was, I got to like him in the end much better than that sappy little prim heroine, his wife. I think one ought to try to get to know one's characters well enough so that their faults are visible as well as their virtues, their charm in spite of their sins. One of the many merits of the characters in the novels of C. P. Snow is this quality of being in the round: Roy Calvert, with his devastating destructiveness and his ineffable charm; Jago, with his ebulliency and his insecurity, his steady devotion to his awful wife, his easily hurt feelings; Sheila with her neurotic self-absorption and queer bursts of honesty. Snow is full of characters who contradict themselves, just as real people *do* contradict themselves. But these are not journalistic portraits; these are artfully constructed characters. They are not alive in the real world, they are alive in the world of fiction.

Free yourself from the facts about the person you may be basing your character on. The facts about him are of little use to you. Make up your own facts. Facts from life will get you nowhere in fiction. Only through your imagination can you touch universality.

One help in freeing a character from real life is to do a process of free association from the person in real life from whom you may have started. I once wanted to write a story about a salty old lady in Connecticut — a real one. After a while I realized she so to speak *meant* the same thing to me as another lady in Virginia. She even looked the same. Then I met a California old lady who was the same type, and filled in. Most people, you will find, do have prototypes in one's memory.

If you make associations thus that lead you four or five or more people away from your starting point, you will find that with each step your character accrues more traits of his own. He is becoming more and more himself — not anyone real, but himself; unique. On the occasions when I am accused of putting a real person into a story, my reaction has come to be that of failure. To that degree I have failed to create a character. I have failed to improve on life — and all writers know that they can improve on life!

The technique of building character is, I think, like all sublimation, the result of frustrating the simple predatory instincts. Those people who stand up for compulsive writing — and there are quite a lot of them — speak as though being an artist necessarily implied being destructive, and so much the worse for the layman. I think that destructiveness *is* the other side of the coin of creativeness, but it seems to me that destructiveness, frustrated and used, can become that critical, analytical discipline which is exactly what the artist needs for his work, exactly what Wolfe for instance needed. Discipline was what he was seeking when he went to Perkins; when he left him, he was seeking self-discipline.

Destruction is exactly what it does feel like to a writer when someone proposes that he pare and chisel at his miraculous brainchild that sprang so whole, so golden, into his mind. To Wolfe, who was not given to false modesty, any such paring and chiseling of his characters felt like sacrilege. Of course the first onset of an idea for a character must be like a great surge, a throb, a drive. But this would be only the beginning. We might put the law this way: *Compulsive writing is for first drafts.*

Toward the end of his life, as he neared death at the age of thirty-eight, Wolfe himself believed that he was maturing. He said, "The central character of my new novel will be, in his own experience, every one of us, not merely the sensitive

young fellow in conflict, not merely the sensitive young fellow
in love, but all of these things, and much more, insofar as they
illustrate man's progress and discovery of life, and as they illustrate the world itself, not merely in terms of personal and self-
centred conflict with the world, but in terms of ever-increasing
discovery of life and the world, with a consequent diminution
of the more personal and self-centered vision. . . . I began to
write," he went on, "with an intense and passionate concern
with the designs and purposes of my own youth; that preoccupation has now changed to an intense and passionate concern
with the designs and purposes of life. I think my interests have
turned more and more from the person who is writing the book
to the book the person is writing."

I can't imagine a clearer statement of intent to create characters that could be universal. If Wolfe had lived, it is possible
that he would and could have fulfilled his intent, for his creative powers were vast.

Yet intent is not always enough. Last year a young man in
Virginia asked me if I would read the novel he was writing.
With some caution I asked how long it was. It then appeared
that he had not yet written the novel, but had it so firmly in
mind that he felt equipped to discuss it as a *fait accompli*. I
asked him what it was about. "Well," he said, "it's about this
man who represents the intellectual approach. He *is* rationalism, in symbol, and he is married to this woman who symbolizes feeling. The book covers the nine months in which this
child they have conceived is gestating, see, symbolizing the development of mankind through the various stages of evolution,
fish, frog, and so on. The book ends when the child is born, sym-

bolizing the birth of a union of the masculine and feminine principles. Oh, I forgot to say that they live in the South, which of course represents the unconscious."

"Of course," I said. That novel, if it ever got written, would have been so universal it would have been meaningless.

Part of Wolfe's new viewpoint, his biographer tells us, was a realization summed up in his title *You Can't Go Home Again.* In other words, you have to grow up. You cannot go on forever seeking and finding new fathers and new mothers, in turn to be thrown over and destroyed when they no longer can carry the needed symbol. It was a sound realization, and it was about time Wolfe had it.

He had dealt with Mrs. Bernstein and with Perkins in his novels to a degree that we would certainly be justified in calling ruthless, since both actually went to him, pleading with him to spare them. Now we see, with the most curious reversal, Wolfe calling these objects of his destructiveness, destructive themselves. It is as if he was unable to accept responsibility for what he himself had insisted upon doing, but had to project it. *Of* Perkins he wrote, "It's as if he wants me to come to grief," and *to* him, "Are you trying to destroy me? Don't you want me to go on? Don't you want me to write another book? Worry, grief and disillusionment have well-nigh destroyed my talent — is this what you wanted?" If it were not so tragic in its wrongheadedness, this cry of Wolfe's would be funny. Perkins, who had been the father Wolfe wanted him to be — who had been incredibly patient, given everything and asked nothing in return except to publish Wolfe's work, after all — is now accused of trying to destroy Wolfe. Wolfe made similar accusations to Mrs. Bernstein. These are comparable to the accusations made by teen-agers who, when they are breaking away from their childhoods, accuse their parents of trying to ruin their lives.

Now, growing up does have its essentially destructive aspect — the necessary destruction of the child behind in order that the adult in front may go forward. Growing up means taking responsibility for one's own acts; but until they can, the young can usually be found blaming everyone in sight for their woes and conflicts. This is all quite normal. But Wolfe was actually an adult, and it is faintly repulsive to hear a grown man accusing those who have befriended him of wishing for his ruin. Instead of becoming responsible for his own potentially useful powers of destruction, he put them off onto his adopted literary and sexual parents.

Wolfe's attitude toward his art, his life, and himself was, for most of his life, that of a child who has not yet grown up to realize everything has two sides. That every fact has a meaning. That every outburst entails some kind of drawing in. That to every massive creative effort there is the complementary negative critical reaction, which in his case was not accepted as such, but voiced itself only in great cries of blind agony and of being misunderstood. For instance, when Wolfe was contemplating the break with Perkins, and was brooding over it on vacation in New Orleans, he got a letter from his lawyer telling him he ought to return to New York to face a suit brought against him by the Dorman family for libel. He suspected Perkins of having given his address to the lawyer — as it proved, without foundation. He wrote to Perkins as follows: "All this worry, grief, and disappointment of the past two years has almost broken me. This final thing was almost the last straw. I was desperately in need of rest and quiet. [The lawyer's] letter destroyed it all, ruined all the happiness and joy I had hoped for." He then once more accuses Perkins of trying to destroy him, this time because of this baseless suspicion that Perkins had given his address to the lawyer, and continues, "All that magnificent and powerful talent I had two years ago, — in the name of God is that to be lost entirely, destroyed under the repeated assaults and criminalities of this blackmail society? Now I know what happens to the artist in America. I shall work for the abolition of the vile and rotten system under which we live."

This may be the cry of an artist, but it is not the cry of a man. As a matter of fact, what it is the cry of is a compulsive writer who has not realized that the other side of compulsiveness is judgment. To those who successfully blockade themselves against judgment, judgment comes unaware, with a sense of horror. The other side of day is dark night. The other side of creation is to draw back, to criticize, and to order. Wolfe never found his other side. His work seemed to him sacrosanct. He was so unwilling to entertain any criticism of it even from himself that he projected his dark side onto Perkins and Mrs. Bernstein. Nothing was his own fault. The dark side seemed continually to be surprising him, filling him with horror, as of the Devil, who appeared always to be on the other side.

I would be prepared to accept all this unawareness as fine if it had worked; but as we all know it did not work. Wolfe died at thirty-eight of tuberculosis of the brain; the doctor who operated said his brain was "covered with simply millions of tubercles." At the very time when he had cut loose from his father Perkins, and was prepared to face the fact that he could not go home again — was, in short, ready to grow up — he died.

{ 64 }

When I finished reading the biography of Wolfe, the overpowering impression I carried away was of all the pain and suffering Wolfe brought upon himself and upon others. There is such a vast amount of anguish in his life, and so little human understanding or compassion. He gave the world many beautiful things, but he could not give himself even the awareness of his own latent critical powers. Rather, he seems to have overwhelmed awareness by continuing to write, compulsively, more and more and more, into the millions of words.

At the beginning of this section I spoke of hoping to be able to pass on some of the things which I feel stand in a writer's way and impede him when he tries to construct characters that will live in his readers' memories. I do feel one of these impediments can be not to grow up above, transcend, the compulsion to write of life first crack out of the box. Let me urge young writers — free yourself of facts. Free yourself of the actual literal events of real people's lives. Use the imagination God gave you. Say an inner no to outside reality, and then let your imagination do what it loves most to — embroider habits and adventures around a fictitious person plucked, sure enough, out of real life, but, by the process of accruing, grown into an individual. Say no to the way things really are, and you will find that that refusal grows into a new condition, a new set of circumstances. Say no to the way your first draft comes out, and see how your rejection of compulsive writing makes ideas issue forth in new ways, alternative expressions.

The fact is that the imagination thrives on frustration. Bottle it up here and it will crop out there, three times as strong. Don't treat your imagination as if it were a weak fragile thing to be pampered. It's not. Refuse it one thing and it will grab another. This is to use discipline; this is to use control. This kind of saying no is the essential condition for creating anything at all.

What it all comes down to is that you, as a writer, have got to accept responsibility for what you write. Who else will? You can, if you choose, be a poor helpless thing in the power of your overmastering creative urge. You can be a poor helpless thing that has to write everything just as inspiration first dictated, devoid of critical judgment, without the freedom of using your powers to select or reject. Or you can, if you choose, and if you work at it, become master of your creative urge. Not thwarting it, guiding it; making it serve you.

This doesn't for a moment mean that you should deny the truth as it speaks in your artistic vision. Your vision is true, it is your real self; but it can become more true if it is helped to fulfill itself with time instead of jumping the gun with it. Don't compromise your original vision; enlarge it.

For art is not overwhelming drive or the helpless submission to phantasy, but, as Webster puts it, "Human contrivance or ingenuity, as in adapting natural things to man's use." What I am urging is that adaptation. As Philip Rieff says in *Freud: The Mind of the Moralist*, "Literature is the guile some personalities develop in exhibiting their deeper emotions."

{ *FIVE* }

The Novel: A Passage to Relationship

POSSIBLY what has made the novel so perennially fascinating a form to generations of readers is that it is so much like real life, made up like life of interacting relationships between all degrees of conflicting mentalities, classes, races, types, maturities, moralities; like real life, but at one remove.

T. S. Eliot says that humankind cannot bear very much reality, and that might account to their turning to the novel. Or, to put it a little differently, it may be that what humankind cannot bear directly it *can* bear indirectly and from a safe distance. Life, that exhausting, alarming, fascinating, bewildering business, can be tasted without pain or untoward consequence through the reading of novels — which might explain why novels outsell collections of short stories as they do. A good novel is one which successfully simulates life, some kind of life. One of the great gifts of the novel to man is that through reading it he can in the end have lived not merely his own lone life but many and diverse others.

E. M. Forster in *Aspects of the Novel* says, "We cannot un-

Given in 1960 at the Cosmopolitan Club, New York City.

{ 67 }

derstand each other except in a rough and ready way; we cannot reveal ourselves, even when we want to; what we call intimacy is only makeshift; perfect knowledge is an illusion. But in the novel we can know people perfectly and apart from the general pleasure of reading; we can find here a compensation for their dimness, in life. In this, fiction is truer than history, because it goes beyond the evidence; and each of us knows from his own experience that there *is* something beyond the evidence; and even if the novelist has not got it correctly — well, he has tried."

The elements within the novel which seem to me most useful for conveying this illusion of life are those of time, scene, and character. Also, the illusion of life is best rendered when it is supported, just as real lives are, by a framework of purpose which, in the novel, is called theme. If the theme is a valid and absorbing one it will support what rests on it. In addition to all these in rendering the illusion of life in the novel are the tricks of magic which the good novelist must perform; as William Maxwell says, "The writer must have everything in common with the vaudeville magician except this: the writer must be taken in by his own tricks. Having practiced incessantly for five, ten, fifteen or twenty years, he must begin by pleasing himself. If he is a good writer you can lean against his trees; they will not give way."

The theme of any story, perhaps especially the novel, is something that has somehow to be got from the writer's mind into the reader's with a minimum of friction, as by osmosis. The novelist must learn what tricks will best accomplish this. The mere fact that he has a good story; the fact that he is burning to tell it; even the fact that it concerns something important —

none of all this matters unless it can be put across to the reader so that the reader burns with its goodness and importance too. Fortunately, writers differ from ordinary daydreamers, if only because they do have this urge to convey their imaginings to the minds of other people.

No larger theme has been attempted in the novel of our time than that of Forster's *A Passage to India*. It is the universally applicable theme of separateness, division; of the splitting so characteristic of this world since Luther, so obviously the cause of all our woes, so apparently irredeemable. In *A Passage to India* we are shown the separation of race from race, religion from religion, sex from sex, caste from caste, and, most significantly of all, friend from friend. As Lionel Trilling has pointed out, throughout this great bellwether novel runs the device of the echo. To every sound, to every happening, there is an echo to plague its characters. Real echoes are heard, also imaginary echoes. Actions or speeches of the characters are later echoed in faintly varied forms. Characters themselves have echoes in other characters. Every virtue has its negative echo; every vice its separate echo of ironic good.

Division, separateness, is of course an opposite to relationship; and relationship is, I believe, the proper concern of the novel. Frank O'Connor says, "I have small doubt that the subject of a novel is almost invariably the relation of the individual to society." But what is relationship? People are always talking about their relationship with this person and that; with their aunt, or their dentist, or their divorced wife's new husband. Do they know what they are talking about?

Webster defines relationship as the state of being related, by kindred, affinity, or other alliance. To be related, he further says, is to stand in relation or connection; to be connected by blood or alliance, especially by consanguinity, which in turn means. blood; kinship. And kinship means, in that charming fashion by which the dictionary brings you back to where you started, relationship.

In what I say about *A Passage to India* I am going to try to exhibit not merely relationships as we experience them in the pages of this novel. I want to exhibit something in *A Passage to India* which I believe is to be found there — a sort of definition, made through the novel's action, of relationship itself. I believe that *A Passage to India* is concerned not only with relationships, but is *about* relationship. My hope is that through an understanding of what Forster says about relationship in his novel, we may better understand that which is the material of all novels, or perhaps I might even say of all fiction.

Upon a vast and unassailably valid framework Forster has constructed an illusion so similar to real life, so comparable to a real world, that it is worth examining it in detail to see how such illusions are effected. Forster is, of course, the master trickster of our literary century, the novelist who rides so easy in the stirrups, so light in the saddle, that he can turn around and do the unforgivable — pull the reader up on the pommel with such asides as (in another novel); "Rickie began to relate his history. The reader who has no book will be obliged to listen to it." Yet never for one instant in Forster do we lose the sense of life, point, meaning, without which the finest plot in the world is so much pulp paper and graphite.

The plot of *A Passage to India*, which figures forth its theme, is, briefly, that a young English lady, Adela Quested, comes to India chaperoned by the elderly Mrs. Moore to see

Ronny, Adela's fiancé and Mrs. Moore's son by a first marriage. Both are liberal, both shocked by the arrogance of the ruling British and repelled by Ronny's manner in assuming the white man's burden. Mrs. Moore goes, against convention, into a mosque one evening and there makes acquaintance with Dr. Aziz, a young Moslem, who is bitterly snubbed and hurt by and at odds with the British. Through him comes Mrs. Moore's and Adela's chance to know "the real India." Aziz organizes an expedition to the Marabar Caves, in one of which Mrs. Moore has an upsetting psychic experience with its echo. In another cave, Adela has the hallucination that, in the darkness, Aziz has attempted to rape her. At her accusation the entire British community is fired to heroic rage. Only Fielding, the local college principal, and Mrs. Moore are not convinced of Aziz's guilt, but perceive that Adela is the victim of a delusion. Fielding is ostracized for his championship of the native, and Ronny sends his mother away. At the trial, Adela suddenly realizes the hallucinatory nature of her experience and recants. Aziz is cleared, Fielding is promoted, the English colony is furious.

This is the story that the novelist has undertaken to make real for us; and he does so by a combination of creating the tempo of life upon the Indian subcontinent, creating scenes which we can visualize and which stamp themselves upon the mind — a great virtue in the novel, where it is essential to an enjoyment of the whole that one should not forget what has gone before — and his rendering of character. These elements, of course, occur simultaneously, intermeshing with and supplementing one another.

Whenever I myself switch from a period of writing short stories to writing a novel, I find the greatest difficulty in slow-ing down from the crucial tempo of the short story, where everything must be seen at the same time, to the leisurely, reflective, digressive rhythm of the novel, where events take place in logical sequence; in "the rhythm of life itself." Do not misunderstand me. It is not the style, the writing, of short stories which need be staccato. A short story can be written in the most gently flowing of rhythms and yet enmesh the happenings of a whole year in the one event that occurs in it. But its tempo is not that of real life but that of inner decision; the tempo of crisis. A novel, on the other hand, can be written in Hemingway's economical language or in O'Hara's tight idiom and yet preserve the illusion of life as it really happened; not boiled down into a revealing incident at all, but related, seen as it occurred, one event after another. Such a novel will attempt to reproduce the tempo that belongs to its setting, to its characters' mode of thinking and acting — at the points at which tempo, scene, and character intermesh.

Listen to Forster giving the tempo of Moslem life:

[Aziz] too generalized from his disappointments — it is difficult for members of a subject race to do otherwise. Granted the exceptions, he agreed that all Englishwomen are haughty and venal. The gleam passed from the conversation, whose wintry surface unrolled and expanded interminably.

A servant announced dinner. They ignored him. The elder men had reached their eternal politics, Aziz drifted into the garden. The trees smelt sweet — green-blossomed champak — and scraps of Persian poetry came into his head. Dinner, dinner, dinner . . . but when he returned to the house for it, Mahmoud Ali had drifted away in his turn, to speak to his sais. "Come and see my wife a little then," said Hamidullah, and they spent twenty minutes behind the purdah. Hamidullah Begum was a distant aunt of Aziz . . . and she had much to say to him on this occasion about a family circumcision that had been celebrated with imperfect pomp. It was difficult to get away, because until they had had their dinner she would not begin hers, and consequently prolonged her remarks in case they should suppose she was impatient. Having censured the circumcision, she bethought her of kindred topics, and asked Aziz when he was going to be married.

Respectful but irritated, he answered, "Once is enough."

And listen to the following evocation of the British tempo. The two visiting ladies have voiced their request to see something of the real India:

"Miss Quested, what a name!" remarked Mrs. Turton to her husband as they drove away. She had not taken to the new young lady, thinking her ungracious and cranky. She trusted that she hadn't been brought out to marry nice little Heaslop, though it looked like it. Her husband agreed with her in his heart, but he never spoke against an Englishwoman if he could avoid doing so, and he only said that Miss Quested naturally made mistakes. He added: "India does wonders for the judgment, especially during the hot weather; it has even done wonders for Fielding." Mrs. Turton closed her eyes at this name and remarked that Mr. Fielding wasn't pukka, and had better marry Miss Quested, for she wasn't pukka. Then they reached their bungalow, low and enormous, the oldest and most uncomfortable bungalow in the civil station, with a sunk soup plate of a lawn, and they had one drink more, this time of barley water, and went to bed. Their withdrawal from the club had broken up the evening, which, like all gatherings, had an official tinge. A community that bows the knee to a Viceroy and believes that the divinity that hedges a king can be transplanted, must feel some reverence for any viceregal substitute. At Chandrapore the Turtons were little gods; soon they would retire to some suburban villa, and die exiled from glory.

One of the fictional problems which requires most skillful legerdemain is that of presenting a character who is to be good; who is to be in the right. It is far easier to make readers take to your villain than to your hero. If you praise him, he sounds goody-goody. If you reveal him in all his glorious superiority, the reader's sympathy will go sneaking out to his inferiors.

Not enough has been said, in my opinion, about Forster as humorist. I think he is the funniest writer in English. Dr. Aziz in *A Passage to India* constitutes the sort of problem-character of which I am speaking. He is in the right, he is earnest, he is wronged, a combination of traits which would make him an insufferable character if treated seriously. But the success of this novel depends on the reader's being sympathetic to Aziz. Forster solved the problem by making Aziz funny. We can laugh at him, and the more we laugh, the more tenderly we feel.

Listen to a bit of the description of Aziz organizing his picnic to the Caves.

Aziz was terribly worried. . . . Trouble after trouble encountered him. . . .
At last the moment arrived.
His friends thought him most unwise to mix himself up with English ladies, and warned him to take every precaution against unpunctuality. Consequently he spent the previous night at the station. The servants were huddled on the platform, enjoined not to stray. He himself walked up and down . . . He felt insecure and also unreal. A car drove up, and he hoped Fielding would get out of it, to lend him solidity. But it contained Mrs. Moore, Miss Quested, and their Goanese servant. He rushed to meet them, suddenly happy. "But you've come, after all! Oh, how very kind of you!" he cried. "This is the happiest moment in all my life!"

The ladies were civil. It was not the happiest moment in their lives, still, they looked forward to enjoying themselves as soon as the bother of the early start was over. . . .

The night was still dark, but had acquired the temporary look that indicates its end. Perched on the roof of a shed, the station-master's hens began to dream of kites instead of owls. Lamps were put out, in order to save the trouble of putting them out later; the smell of tobacco and the sound of spitting arose from third-class passengers in dark corners; heads were unshrouded, teeth cleaned on the twigs of a tree. So convinced was a junior official that another sun would rise, that he rang a bell with enthusiasm. This upset the servants. They shrieked that the train was starting, and ran to both ends of it to intercede. Much had still to enter the purdah carriage [where the ladies would travel] — a box bound with brass, a melon wearing a fez, a towel containing guavas, a step-ladder, and a gun. The guests played up all right. They had no race-consciousness — Mrs. Moore was too old, Miss Quested too new — and they behaved to Aziz as to any young man who had been kind to them in the country. This moved him deeply. He had expected them to arrive with Mr. Fielding, instead of which they trusted themselves to be with him a few moments alone.

"Send back your servant," he suggested. . . . "Then we shall all be Moslems together."

"And he is such a horrible servant. Antony, you can go; we don't want you," said the girl impatiently.

"Master told me to come."

"Mistress tells you to go."

"Master says, keep near the ladies all morning."

"Well, your ladies won't have you." She turned to the host. "Do get rid of him, Dr. Aziz!"

"Mohammed Latif!" he called.

The poor relative exchanged fezzes with the melon, and peeped out of the window of the railway carriage, whose confusion he was superintending.

"Here is my cousin, Mr. Mohammed Latif. Oh no, don't shake hands. He is an Indian of the old-fashioned sort, he prefers to salaam. There, I told you so. Mohammed Latif, how beautifully you salaam. See, he hasn't understood; he knows no English."

"You spick lie," said the old man gently.

"I spick a lie! Oh, jolly good. Isn't he a funny old man? We will have great jokes with him later. He does all sorts of little things. He is not nearly as stupid as you think, and awfully poor. . . ." He threw one arm round the grubby neck. . . .

He was getting nervous again, for it was ten minutes to the time. Still, Fielding was an Englishman, and they never do miss trains, and Godbole was a Hindu and did not count, and, soothed by this logic, he grew calmer. . . . Mohammed Latif had bribed Antony not to come.

A story which conveys no meaning beyond its overt idea is not only boring but is only half of itself. Meaning can be ignored; indeed, the author can remain ignorant of it. But it is always there. For writers who know it is there, and who wish to convey it to the reader, remains the problem of *how* it is to be conveyed. Sermons are no longer popular reading, and the intelligent reader will shy away like a skittish horse from having meanings pointed out to him. Moreover, the intelligent writer is far too respectful of meaning to go hawking it around the marketplace. He knows that meaning, to mean anything, must do just that: mean, not state. Meaning is inseparable from idea. The idea is the statement; the meaning — is just the meaning of the idea. The choicest tricks in the literary magicians' bags, the ones that can't be bought at all, are the ones that involve meaning.

A Passage to India means a great many things, but I believe there is one meaning that underlies all the others. Let us see if we can catch it in the echo Mrs. Moore heard in the cave at Marabar.

The more she thought over it, the more disagreeable and frightening it became. She minded it much more now than at the time. The crush and the smells [in the cave] she could forget, but the echo began in some indescribable way to undermine her hold on life. Coming at a moment when she chanced to be fatigued, it had managed to murmur, "Pathos, piety, courage — they exist, but are identical, and so is filth. Everything exists, nothing has value." If one had spoken vileness in that place, or quoted lofty poetry, the [echo's] comment would have been the same — "ou-boum." If one had spoken with the tongues of angels and pleaded for all the unhappiness and misunderstanding in the world, past, present, and to come, for all the misery men must undergo whatever their opinion and position, and however much they dodge or bluff — it would amount to the same. . . . Suddenly at the edge of her mind, Religion appeared, poor little talkative Christianity, and she knew that all its divine words from "Let there be Light" to "It is finished" only amounted to "boum."

Of this scrap let me only say it reveals that in the cave's echo, Mrs. Moore has heard something that negates all her values; a balance, an opposite, for everything positive. She feels this to be unbearable.

After Adela has accused Aziz of attempting to rape her in the caves, an atmosphere of heroically controlled hysteria descends over the English community. Let us look at one of the many scenes in which Forster conveys this atmosphere.

People drove into the club with studious calm — the jog-trot of country gentlefolk between green hedgerows, for the natives must not suspect that they were agitated. They exchanged the usual drinks, but everything tasted different, and then they looked out at the palisade of cactuses stabbing the purple throat of the sky;

they realized that they were thousands of miles from any scenery that they understood. The club was fuller than usual, and several parents had brought their children into the rooms reserved for adults, which gave the air of the Residency at Lucknow. One young mother — a brainless but most beautiful girl — sat on a low ottoman in the smoking-room with her baby in her arms; her husband was away in the district, and she dared not return to her bungalow in case the "niggers attacked." The wife of a small railway official, she was generally snubbed; but this evening, with her abundant figure and masses of corn-gold hair, she symbolized all that is worth fighting and dying for; more permanent a symbol, perhaps, than poor Adela. "Don't worry, Mrs. Blakiston, those drums are only Mohurram," the men would tell her. "Then they've started," she moaned, clasping the infant and rather wishing he would not blow bubbles down his chin at such a moment as this. "No, of course not, and anyhow, they're not coming to the club." "And they're not coming to the Burra Sahib's bungalow either, my dear, and that's where you and your baby'll sleep tonight," answered Mrs. Turton, towering by her side like Pallas Athene, and determining in the future not to be such a snob.

Mrs. Moore is one of the only two people who retain the conviction that Aziz has been wrongly accused, and to get rid of her, her son Ronny ships her back to England in all the heat of May. She is too deeply disorganized by that echo, about which she is still brooding, to remonstrate, or to come to Dr. Aziz's aid.

She had come to that state where the horror of the universe and its smallness are both visible at the same time — the twilight of the double vision in which so many elderly people are involved. . . . In the twilight of the double vision, a spiritual muddledom is set up for which no high-sounding words can be found; we can neither act nor refrain from action, we can neither ignore nor respect Infinity. . . . What had spoken to her in that scoured-out cavity of the granite? What dwelt in the first of the caves?

Something very old and very small. Before time, it was before space also. Something snub-nosed, incapable of generosity — the undying worm itself. Since hearing its voice, she had not entertained one large thought. . . . All this fuss over a frightened girl! Nothing had happened, "and if it had," she found herself thinking with the cynicism of a withered priestess, "if it had, there are worse evils than love." The unspeakable attempt presented itself to her as love: in a cave, in a church — Boum, it amounts to the same.

The crisis in *A Passage to India,* or rather, the crisis of all its lesser crises, comes when Adela appears, faint and ill, in court, to testify against Aziz. To cut this scene is on the order of an amputation; nevertheless, I would like to quote a bit of it as an example of *change* — in character and in timing — which is what crisis in a novel implies.

In fiction, when a crisis is dealt with, we have passed over a bridge. We move to the other shore. Something has changed for good.

Adela had always meant to tell the truth and nothing but the truth. . . . As soon as she rose to reply, and heard the sound of her own voice . . . a new and unknown sensation protected her, like magnificent armour. She didn't think what had happened or even remember in the ordinary way of memory, but she returned to the Marabar Hills, and spoke from them across a sort of darkness to Mr. McBryde. The fatal day recurred, in every detail, but now she was of it and not of it at the same time, and this double relation gave it indescribable splendour. . . . The sun rose again, the elephant waited, the pale masses of the rock flowed around her and presented the first cave; she entered . . . Questions were asked, and to each she found the exact reply; yes, she had noticed the "Tank of the Dagger" . . . yes, Mrs. Moore had been tired after the first cave and sat in the shadow of a great rock . . .

"You went alone into one of those caves?"

"That is quite correct."

"And the prisoner followed you." —

"Now we've got 'im," [whispered] the Major.

[Adela] was silent. The court . . . awaited her reply. But she could not give it until [where her mind now was] Aziz entered the place of answer.

"The prisoner followed you, didn't he?" [Mr. McBryde] repeated in the monotonous tones that they both used; they were employing agreed words throughout, so that this part of the proceedings held no surprises.

"May I have half a moment before I reply to that, Mr. McBryde?"

"Certainly."

Her vision was of several caves. She saw herself in one, and she was also outside it, watching its entrance, for Aziz to pass in. She failed to locate him. It was the doubt that had often visited her, but solid and attractive, like the hills. . . . "I am not quite sure."

"I beg your pardon?" said the Superintendent of Police.

"I cannot be sure . . ."

"I didn't catch that answer." He looked scared; his mouth shut with a snap. "You are on that landing, or whatever we term it, and you have entered a cave. I suggest to you that the prisoner followed you."

She shook her head.

"What do you mean, please?"

"No," she said, in a flat, unattractive voice. Slight noises began in various parts of the room, but no one yet understood what was occurring except Fielding. He saw that she was going to have a nervous breakdown and that his friend was saved.

Thus does Forster exhibit the crux of the action in the novel. The event on which all the excitement, both English and Indian, had hinged, the one big fact, was, actually, illusion; a hallucination of Adela's mind. That outrage which had provoked so much heroics, such a parade of English God-Almightiness and of Indian emotionalism, is echoed by a kind of Boum, which says, it never happened at all.

At the book's end, the separations which abound in this novel, all the pairs of opposites, are brought together symbolically in a meeting, some years later, between Aziz and Fielding. Any resolution to the myriad conflicts recognized by the novel we may expect to find here.

Lionel Trilling in his book on Forster queries why Aziz, the principal character to represent the Eastern view, is made a Moslem instead of a Hindu when the book is so "suffused with Hinduism." It may be because the hate and violence of Islam constitute a suitable opposite to the love and busy activity of that Western culture which Fielding, for all his liberality, perforce represents. This pair of opposites, symbolizing all the other pairs of opposites, rides along as Fielding and Aziz guide their horses, side by side, through the Mau jungle.

Forster is an artist, not a reformer nor a prophet, and so any solutions he offers to the repeated problems of separation which he has raised in his novel will not be stated, we may be confident. However, if we ride along in the rear, listening carefully to the conversation as it drifts back to us, there is a chance that we may catch some answers.

The echo in the Indian caves negated Western values no more utterly than the British in this novel have negated Eastern values. And in their last conversation, we hear both Fielding and Aziz negate Hinduism. "Do you know anything about this Krishna business?" Fielding asks. "My dear chap . . . how . . . should it concern you and me?" Aziz replies.

"What I want to discover is its spiritual side, if it has one," Fielding says.

"It is useless discussing Hindus with me. . . . Why so curious about them?" Aziz asks.

"It's difficult to explain." Fielding answers. . . . "Why do my wife and her brother like Hinduism? . . . They won't talk to me about this."

Fielding has married a daughter of Mrs. Moore's, and Mrs. Moore, who died on the voyage back to England, was curiously sacred to Aziz, a sort of unifying symbol between East and West.

"Oh, shut up," Aziz says now, however. "Don't spoil our last hour with foolish questions. Leave Krishna alone, and talk about something sensible."

What *do* these men consider sensible, as they discuss a solution to the East-West problem?

Fielding thinks, about his wife, "There seemed a link between them at last — that link outside either participant that is necessary to every relationship." To the Westerner, an inheritor of the Christian tradition, it is Love, this outside link of interpersonal relationship that is Fielding's only answer to the problem.

Aziz's solution to the problem, as a Moslem, is for the English to clear out of India. "Clear out, you fellows, double quick, I say. . . . We shall drive every blasted Englishman into the sea, and then . . . you and I shall be friends." Only by nationalism, which is a sort of mass egotism, can the problem be solved.

" 'Why can't we be friends now?' " Fielding asks. " 'It's what I want. It's what you want.' But the horses didn't want it —

they swerved apart; the earth didn't want it, sending up rocks through which riders must pass single file." Nature is not willing to go along "now" with either the Christian or the Moslem solution, at least not Nature in this Hindu ground over which they ride. Is there a solution to the problem of separateness offered in that Hindu thought which both riders have just dismissed with such contempt?

Krishna, Brahman's incarnation, says, in the Bhagavad-Gita: "This entire universe is pervaded by me, in that eternal form of mine which is not manifest to the senses. Although I am not within any creature, all creatures exist within me. I do not mean that they exist within me physically. That is my divine mystery. My Being sustains all creatures, and brings them to birth, but has no physical contact with them.

> *My face is equal*
> *To all creation*
> *Loving no one*
> *Nor hating any.*"

The God of the Hindus is a god of being, without attributes. It is far from being the god of extinction that Trilling appears to imagine. "That which is non-existent can never come into being," Krishna says, "and that which is, can never cease to be. Bodies are said to die, but that which possesses the body is eternal." In the Bhagavad-Gita, relationship is seen to consist in the acceptance of relationship.

Mrs. Moore could not accept the answering echo. Aziz cannot accept the West. The English could not accept that Miss Quested's experience could be all an illusion. If that was illusion, how much else in their whole situation might also be illusion? Nobody in the book, saving the Hindu Professor God-bole, can accept the premise upon which Hindu philosophy is based, that everything in the universe has, so to speak, an echo, and that echo, its echo; that opposites exist to everything, and because they exist, are mutually related. The fact of the existence of two opposed things *is* the relationship between them.

Aziz and Fielding, by this view of life which they reject — but which we may suspect their creator, Forster, accepts — may not be able to be friends; neither need they be enemies. Since both exist, they are already related; the relationship is there and needs only to be accepted. But that they cannot do, riding past "the temples, the tank, the jail, the palace, the birds, the carrion, the Guest House, that came into view as they issued from the gap and saw Mau beneath: they didn't want it, they said in their hundred voices, 'No, not yet,' and the sky said, 'No, not there.' "

I think myself that Forster is suggesting, in the culminating words of a book which is all suggestion, that behind the Moslem God, and the Christian God, sits enthroned a God of acceptance, who embraces all things, not because they are sensible, or admirable or right, or pitiable, or lovable, or in any way worthy, but simply because he is, and they are.

SIX

Hemingway and the Courage to Be

I REMEMBER as a very young writer being advised by a much older and very wise one to write not about myself, but about the universal. My reaction to this advice was one of pure horror. At that stage of my life, which was in my own twenties and the century's thirties, what universal meant to me in terms of literature was a picture of great Knut Hamsun types plodding up and down a hill day after day carrying heavy burdens which they laid down only in order to make a bestial version of love interspersed with inarticulate grunts. What universal meant to me then was boringness beyond the dreams of avarice; and what I wanted most on earth, both in my life and in my writing, was not to be boring.

This, of course, for the young writer of that day involved an enormous outlay of energy all down the line; one had stringently to edit oneself, both in conversation and on paper, so as to achieve an effect of toughness and unconventionality. One had to concern one's life and one's writing with the strange, the picturesque, and the somewhat improper. In those days the epitome of what was not boring, for both young writers and

young readers, was Ernest Hemingway's *The Sun Also Rises,*
which seemed to us to express to the *n*th degree the strange,
the picturesque, and the improper. The thing we wanted most
to achieve was novelty — the individual, the different. I am
afraid that the advice about writing about the universal went
in one ear and, if not out the other, got lost somewhere in between.

Hemingway said somewhere, "There are some things which
cannot be learned quickly; and time, which is all we have,
must be paid heavily for their acquiring. They are the very
simplest things, and because it takes a man's life to know them,
the little new that each man gets from life is very costly, and
the only heritage he has to leave." One of the things, far from
new, that must be acquired by a writer in the course of his experience is the knowledge that he can just stop worrying over
whether he is expressing his individual self in his writing; it is
impossible, one gradually perceives over the years, not to do so.
Whether the writer chooses Africa as a setting for his work, or
outer space, whether his characters are bankers, prostitutes, or
skin-divers, on its deepest level, ultimately, his work will concern the problem of himself, though he take the wings of the
morning and dwell in the uttermost parts of the sea. Many
writers have to some degree or another realized this largely
involuntary perception of the ordinarily unperceivable which
take place along with the production of fiction. Flaubert said
that he was Emma Bovary, but Emma Bovary was, likewise, he.

It doesn't seem to me to make too much difference whether
you abhor the universal in literature or adore it; whether you
think of it as meaning to plod knee-deep through mud or as a
kind of symbolism that is devoid of all humanity. What matters

in either of these cases is that you have not grasped its practical meaning at all. The Oxford English Dictionary has columns devoted to narrowing down the meaning of the word "universal," but I think that for our relatively limited purposes of taking a short look at universality in themes for fiction, we might begin with the premise that in fiction, universality means: true of human experience in general. I suggest we hold this yardstick up against a number of pieces of fiction and consider them from this point of view.

In the cabin where I wrote this section, there were a number of last year's women's magazines — publications whose avowed purpose is to give their readers stories that are, in the words of one of the magazines, "about you and your life." This intent would certainly seem to aim at universality. Yet one of the days when I was thinking up reasons for not going to work I read one of the stories in one of the magazines. It was by Faith Baldwin. It was very short. It was about a modern young couple who have a girl baby and then have a boy baby, and worry themselves sick that the first baby will become jealous of the second baby if the first baby does not receive extra attention. Jealousy, they fear, will lead to neurosis, if not to actual delinquency. So the little girl gets all their attention and babying, until the children's grandparents begin to worry too — that the little boy will get to be the neurotic one. But as the grandparents watch one evening, the little girl takes away the little boy's toy — as usual unchided. The little boy gets to his feet, toddles across the room, and with another toy hits the little girl on the head. He then takes back his original toy. The grandfather, beaming, says, "He'll do. He's in." The end.

I suppose that is true of a kind of human experience. The

characters live in New Jersey, belong to the affluent society, are in normal health; the thing they are all worrying about, sibling rivalry, is a legitimate problem. The point of the story — that we don't need to worry so much about our children because on the whole they can take care of themselves — is sound. Yet I cannot say that I consider this story to possess universality. For one thing, it sets up the sound enough problem of sibling rivalry only to negate it by, in effect, saying, Oh, well, there isn't any problem anyway. For another its moment of crisis, when the little boy hits the little girl over the head with the toy, has no comprehensive conclusive meaning: it could just as well herald the *onset* of delinquency in the little boy. To be universal, such moments of crisis must find their expression in a symbolic event of sufficient power to embrace the unique and separate experiences of both characters and of author. The crucial episode in the Baldwin story is not such a symbolic event. I would say the story demonstrates only that a writer can concern himself with the average and the normal, and produce solutions to familiar problems, without coming anywhere near the universal.

On the bookstand beside the cabin table on which I was writing, along with the OED, Fowler, and Roget's Thesaurus, were a few novels, among them *Lolita*. I first read *Lolita* in an edition a friend bought for me in Switzerland and brought in while the book was still banned in America. He told me that the bookseller in Berne, an Englishman, while looking down his nose at him had delivered a severe lecture about the goods he was nevertheless taking money for — declaring that the book was obscene, immoral, in opposition to all normal, healthy decency. That is not the way *Lolita* strikes me. While its author disclaims, in perhaps unnecessarily emphatic tones, interest in or admiration for psychoanalysis, one does not need to have read very much Freud to recognize in *Lolita* one of the underlying themes of human psychology, spread out like a patient etherized upon a table — in much the same way and in much the same spirit that the great themes of the Greek tragedies lie spread out for us to analyze and dissect (and fail to break down to even the slightest degree).

Lolita is almost unbearably moving in its unfolding of a human love born out of unspeakable lust. It is no syrupy woman's-magazine remorse that Nabokov describes, as his protagonist, waiting for the police to come and arrest him for the murder of the other corrupter of Lolita's youth, remembers a day soon after he lost her when he stood on a mountainside looking down over a town and "behind it all, great timbered mountains. But even brighter than those quietly rejoicing colors, both brighter and dreamier to the ear than they were to the eye, was that vapory vibration of accumulated sounds that never ceased for a moment, as it rose to the lip of granite where I stood wiping my foul mouth. And soon I realized that all these sounds were of one nature, that no other sounds than these came from the streets of the transparent town, with the women at home and the men away. Reader! What I heard was but the melody of children at play; nothing but that; and so limpid was the air that within this vapor of blended voices one could hear now and then, as if released, an almost articulate spurt of vivid laughter, or the crack of a bat, or the clatter of a toy wagon. I stood listening to that musical vibration from my lofty slope, to those flashes of separate cries with a kind of demure murmur for background; and then I knew that the hopelessly poignant thing was not Lolita's absence from my side, but the absence of her voice from that concord." And again, when Humbert Humbert is looking at the pregnant Lolita in the house of her young mechanic husband, "There she was, my Lolita; hopelessly worn at seventeen, and I looked and looked at her and knew as clearly as I know I am to die, that I loved her more than anything I had ever seen or imagined on earth, or hoped for anywhere else. She was only the echo of the nymphet . . . but thank God it was not that echo alone that I worshiped. What I used to pamper in my heart, *mon grand péché radieux,* had dwindled to its essence; you may jeer at me and threaten to clear the court . . . but I insist the world know how much I loved my Lolita, *this* Lolita, pale and polluted, and big with another's child. No matter even if those eyes of hers would fade to myopic fish — even then I would go mad with tenderness at the mere sight of your dear wan face, at the mere sound of your raucous young voice, my Lolita."

A Humbert can say this at the end of the novel, who at the beginning of it had been viciously contemptuous of physical maturity in women. Of course it is not every adult, not every parent, who can thus try himself in the court of self-knowledge and pass sentence on the crime we all still commit against those we love best and most purely though less consciously than Humbert. Nabokov has, I believe, in *Lolita* said something about the nature of parental passion and what our possessiveness does to our children and at the same time to the poor child that weeps within us, which is as important as Faith Baldwin's story is unimportant. In saying it, Nabokov demonstrates, for our purposes here, that a writer need not be concerned with the normal or the average to succeed in saying something which is true of important human experience in general. He has concerned himself with passion, with remorse, with the ego, and with love; and as long as there are human beings it is probable that there will be passion, remorse, ego, and love.

Is *Lolita* immoral? Well, what do we mean by moral? A young woman who comes from the Bible belt said that she considered a novel of mine, *The Prodigal Women*, immoral. I asked her what she meant by immoral and she said, "Well, I don't think those women behaved in a very virtuous way." She was quite right; they didn't. But I don't think my novel is immoral, and when I was working in that cabin I consulted the OED to see what moral actually means. I found that definition number 1 is: "Of, or pertaining to, character or disposition; of, or pertaining to, the distinction between right and wrong, or good and evil, in relation to actions, volitions, or character." *Lolita* can certainly be said to be concerned with practically nothing else *but* the distinction between right and wrong, good and evil, in relation to actions, volitions and character. It is not, if you like, conventional; its events do not conform to anything familiar to us in ordinary life; yet it has a terrible moral reality which, I think, makes it possible for us to expand our definition so that we may say that universality in fiction means dealing with the distinction between right and wrong in important human experience.

Another of the qualities which, in my youth, made *The Sun Also Rises* so admired by young writers was that it concerned expatriatism. In that day, to be an expatriate seemed to sum up the very essence of cutting loose from outworn tradition, of asserting one's individuality, and of selecting freely from the countries of the world one's preferred environment. An expatriate, liberated from the confining bonds of family and country, is able to exist as nearly as possible independently, an island entire of himself. A very amusing article about *The Sun Also Rises,* published in the thirties and entitled "Babes in the Bois," described how the novel set a dozen fashions for behavior among the young of those days — how it made it fashionable to talk Hemingwayese, to drink too much, to sleep around, and most of all how terribly, terribly fashionable it became to be unhappy.

Actually, the unhappiness of the two principal characters in *The Sun Also Rises,* Jake and Brett, arises from the rather less fashionable condition of Jake's being sexually crippled by a wartime wound, and from the rather more familiar human condition of frustration. There is no reason advanced anywhere in the novel why if Jake had been sexually normal, Brett should not have stopped sleeping around; why she and Jake should not have been united; and why they should not have been, at least on this score, perfectly happy. The wound, and Jake's resulting incapacity, are responsible for the theme of love's frustration which is the mainspring of the novel's action. Viewing the novel from a distance of thirty years, we may describe it as concerning the frustration of love between man and woman in a setting of almost total absence of conventional moral values, a setting foreign to all the principal characters who move against its backdrop. The setting is so foreign, in fact, and they stand out in such relief against it, that the reader has the unusual opportunity of regarding theme and action of this important book in its author's development as if it were a jigsaw puzzle called "A Problem in Hemingway," with all the pieces present but unassembled; or as a police-court reenactment of a crime in which all details are included to make it possible for the attentive observer to guess the identity of the criminal — in this case, the identity of that causal wartime wound.

Now the difference is vast between a writer who, like the young man in Virginia mentioned in another section, thinks of a novel in terms of its symbols, and a great artist. "When writing a novel," Hemingway has said, "a writer should create living people. People; not characters." Such a great writer would never put the sea into a novel in order to represent the unconscious, or set a boat upon it to represent man's perilous crossing. He, rather, would write about real people in a real ship, things which are real for him in some inner vision that excites him, that means something to him. Any such meaning, however, he would trust to be conveyed within the art; he would not put the art within the meaning. His symbols arise from within, below, in back; are not plucked from outside, above, in front. If his work expresses his own deepest reality it will fit macrocosmic reality as well. This spontaneous gushing up of symbols, as opposed to the imposition of symbols from without, is one of the differences between what is creative and what reductive; between synthesis and analysis. Creative art builds up from within; critical analysis, such as I am attempting here, of Hemingway's expatriatism, takes apart from the outside.

The young poet Arthur Freeman has this to say about expatriatism:

The knife-nosed liner swabs slick oil
across the sunrise. Waves recoil,

cut quick, cut deep — as cruel a knife
severs my living from my life.

The sense of severing, the split, lesion, or wound, has provided the theme for work as various in degree and extent of awareness as — to mention only the books that confronted me from that cabin bookshelf — *Lucky Jim* and *On the Road; Anna Karenina* and *A View of the Harbor;* the poems of W. H. Auden and T. S. Eliot, and *A Passage to India.* The split is present in Forster's twilight of the double vision, in the ironic ignorance Elisabeth Taylor uses to separate the realities; in Auden's divided sea. It is also Eliot's Shadow — between the idea and the reality, between the motion and the act (among other things); since there is a split between all pairs of things that can be seen to be opposed. Of course, in a sense, the split can also be said not to exist, since, as split, it would represent non-being between two entities that are. But then, evil can also be said (though rashly) not to exist.

Now it is my belief that the proper field for ideas for novels, as opposed to ideas for short stories, is the field of relationships — between a number of separate individuals, between races or classes or sexes, most of all between the individual and society. The short story, on the other hand, in Frank O'Connor's words, finds its sources in "The profound and common interests of life — the little servant girl so weary of her nursing that she smothers the baby; the cabman so obsessed by his son's death that, when none of his busy customers will listen to him, he tells it to his old cab horse." The short story deals with the individual in relation to himself. We have seen in earlier sections that the short story ranges round a personal circle, bearing in upon it, not outward upon society as does the novel.

Hemingway's first book to be published in a trade edition was a collection, called *In Our Time*, which contains a number of short stories about the boy Nick, who grows up in the American West, the son of a doctor father and an ailing mother; who has a friend Bill and a girl Marjorie. In the stories as collected, each is preceded, as though by some private association of the author's, with a short paragraph dealing with events much later in the century, principally in wartime. If we accept the premise that a short story is contained within its own crisis, and that a crisis represents a decision; if we recognize that an individual is in effect the sum total of all his decisions; then we are at the very least able to reach some idea of what Nick, the total character who emerges from these short stories, is like. There are indications which could lead the reader to assume that Nick is the same boy who later became Jake in *The Sun Also Rises*, Lieutenant Henry in *A Farewell to Arms,* and Robert Jordan in *For Whom the Bell Tolls*. But such connections are unnecessary. For our purposes it is enough that they are all male characters of Hemingway's. They are all aspects of the male personality, viewed in different phases, under different circumstances, by the same author. In Nick, the reader is shown a boy among the early influences that were brought to bear upon his emotional development, making the choices he was led to make under those particular stresses.

In the first of the stories, "Indian Camp," Nick watches his father deliver an Indian woman — whose labor is excruciatingly prolonged and painful — of a baby boy. It is Nick's first view of birth and of death, of man's destiny and of woman's, and represents the boy's formative impression of these opposite poles as an inordinately shocking one. The story ends, "Sitting in the stern of the boat with his father rowing, he felt quite sure that he would never die." The associated paragraph which preceded this story was concerned with moving up to the front in the First World War, that is to say, to the conflict.

The next story, "The Doctor and the Doctor's Wife," gives a picture of the father and of the mother as Nick experienced them. The Doctor is accused of having stolen some driftwood logs by the Indian he has hired to saw them up. In a rage he goes to the bedroom, where his wife, resting, gives him sentimental, moralistic counsel about his problem, much tinged with religiosity. She tells her husband to ask Nick to come to her where she lies in the darkened room. The Doctor goes outdoors. Nick is reading, leaning against a tree. "Your mother wants you to come and see her," the Doctor says. "I want to go with you," Nick says. In a story that is associated, through its preliminary paragraph, with the evacuation of a city in wartime, Nick is seen choosing the part of the father and rejecting the mother. Male values are here equated with the estimable, sincere, and realistic, if morally faulty; female, or feeling, values with the perfectionistic, pretentious, and phony.

The following story, "The End of Something," is prefixed by a paragraph describing the shooting of Germans at Mons. Its narrative concerns a Nick grown somewhat older, and his girl Marjorie, fishing together on the lake. They are involved in a romantic understanding, but as they sit beside a fire together later, on shore, Nick says, "It isn't any fun any more. Not any of it." "Isn't love any fun?" Marjorie says. "No," Nick says. Marjorie rows away in the boat. In a little while Nick, lying with his face buried in the blanket beside the fire, hears Bill coming. "Did she go all right?" Bill asks. "Yes," Nick says.

The choice thus repeated, of the values which male action represents as opposed to the values of feeling and love, was not an easy one, as is stressed by the next story, "The Three Day Blow." Nick and Bill get tight together beside the cabin fire and discuss Nick's having jilted Marjorie. "You were very wise, to bust off that Marge business," Bill says. "Once a man's married, he's absolutely bitched. Married men are done for." "Sure," Nick says. But inwardly he is in the depths. "All he knew was that he had once had Marjorie and that he had lost her. She was gone and he had sent her away. That was all that mattered." The paragraph that prefixes this story concerns severe defeat in battle. It begins to emerge that between the opposite poles of father and mother, of man and woman, of action and feeling — which are equated almost as good and evil — a breach has been made within Nick which, in the absence of any reconciling principle in the given material at hand other than the repeated association with war, death, and defeat — all destruction — we will not be straining a point to call a split or wound.

Of the remaining stories about Nick in this collection, one, "The Battler," is about an old prize-fighter Nick meets when he is thrown off a freight train riding the rails, and starts to camp in the woods. The old man announces he is crazy, and indeed a little later he takes offense at something innocent Nick has said and tries in a frenzy to beat him up. He has said earlier, "When you're crazy you don't know about it." An equation is suggested throughout the whole story between fighting and insanity (that is to say, loss of consciousness or sickness) which, in view of Hemingway's lasting concern with war and fighting, should interest us. The paragraph attached to this story concerns the wartime execution of a cabinet minister who is sick with typhoid — who also is not a well man.

The story that follows it is called "A Very Short Story," and is prefixed by a paragraph which this time serves as the source of information about Nick himself, who is shown in it badly wounded in the war, saying to the friend who lies wounded beside him, "You and me, we've made a separate peace." Being wounded, then (that is, getting out of the collective conflict involuntarily), is an honorable avenue to peace. The succeeding story is about an unnamed American soldier in the Italian army, who falls in love and sleeps with his night nurse while he is hospitalized with a wound. They expect to be married as soon as an armistice is declared and the man can go home and find a job. Their projected union is never effected, however, for after the man goes to America the girl falls in love with an Italian major ("She had never known Italians before") and writes the man that theirs had been only a boy-and-girl love. But the Italian major never does marry her, and the American contracts gonorrhea riding in a taxi with a shopgirl in Chicago. Let us note in passing that this is, in part, the plot of *A Farewell to Arms*, the novel Hemingway wrote after *The Sun Also Rises*, and with which we will presently be concerned.

"Cross Country Snow," in which Nick and a friend, George, go skiing together in Switzerland, is the first of the Nick stories to introduce the idea of expatriation. It is associated with a paragraph that concerns the courage necessary to the art of bullfighting. In the story itself the young men are discussing America, to which Nick must soon return while his wife has a baby.

"Do you want to go?" George says.

"No," Nick says.

"Does your wife?"

"No."

"The mountains aren't much in the States," George says.

"No," Nick says. "They're too rocky. There's too much timber, and they're too far away."

"I wish we were Swiss," George says. "Maybe we'll never go skiing again."

Nick replies, "We've got to. It isn't worth while if you can't." Nick, who has already rejected what the mother represents, and what a relation with the girl he loves represents, here rejects what mother-country represents, and chooses a preferable, a foreign world.

The collection ends with a two-part story, "Big Two-Hearted River," about a grown-up Nick who has lived away, but has now returned to the country of his childhood to fish its streams. Each of the two sections of the story is prefixed by a paragraph that describes the moment of death — one in a bull-ring, the other in a jail. The story offers one of Hemingway's most characteristic pictures of sport, of country, of everything encountered by the physical senses, a picture set against land that has been all burned over since Nick's boyhood.

Through it, Nick hikes. He makes camp. He cooks. He eats beside the campfire. He sleeps. This is the end of the first part, the one prefixed by the paragraph about the art, the dash, and the courage of bull-fighting. In the second part, Nick makes breakfast, wades the stream, fishes, catches two enormous trout, eats lunch. He contemplates going on fishing that afternoon in the swamp beyond. But "Nick did not want to go in there now. He felt a reaction against deep wading. . . . In the swamp, fishing was a tragic adventure. Nick did not want it." Instead, he cleans the two fish. "When he held them back up in the water they looked like real fish. Their color was not gone yet." He starts to return to camp, looks back, and thinks, "There were plenty of days coming when he could fish the swamp."

In the title, with its arresting image of a river with a double heart; in the fact of there being two sections; in the emphasis upon the two trout — so difficult to catch, so unusually big — our attention is continually drawn in this story to the idea of doubles, of pairs. Its only crisis consists of Nick's decision not to go into the swamp, where "the banks were bare, the big cedars came together overhead, the sun did not come through; in the fast water, deepening under his armpits, the fishing would be tragic." Nick does not want to go any farther, any deeper, into this swamp, which we may equate with the jail of the preliminary paragraph.

Judging from what the other associations between preliminary paragraphs and consequent stories have been, this story is to be associated twice with the idea of the actual moment of death. Instead of going on then, in this second part, Nick retreats to the camp described in the first part, where his physical sensations — eating, sleeping, making fire, cooking — have been so pleasurable and satisfying. If we regard this moment of choice as a moment of death, it must be because it is a moment when further progress along a given flow of life becomes blocked. Anything between the pairs of opposites with which we have repeatedly been presented in "Big Two-Hearted River" would thus be a negative entity; that is to say, a gap, division, or split. The pair of fish, that symbol of the pair of opposites between which Nick must choose, look like live fish. But they are not; they are dead fish.

We have noted in this collection of short stories a plot which was later to develop into Hemingway's great novel *A Farewell to Arms,* the latter plot's only significant change a different but no less tragic ending. We may also find among the crises — the decisions — of the other stories of *In Our Time,* conclusions upon which the structure of *A Farewell to Arms* may be seen to rest. Let us listen to the greatly elaborated plot of this novel as it finally appears, to catch, if possible, any echoes.

The novel's setting is once more a foreign land, Italy in the First World War. Lieutenant Henry, an American attached to the Italian army, falls in love with the beautiful army nurse Catherine Barkley. The affair at once takes on intensity and a fatal urgency. Catherine's earlier fiancé has been killed without her ever having experienced sex; the war is everywhere around them, and there seems no time to be lost. To put it differently, in a foreign, outside world, where those cut off from home are involved in a world conflict, the need for their being united is immediate and imperative. The lieutenant is sent off to see action in which he receives a wound in the knee. This wound is not so bad but that, when he has been returned to a hospital and Catherine nurses him there, he can — unlike Jake of *The Sun Also Rises* — enjoy a passionate affair, with a friendly accomplice to guard the door. On his recovery, Lieutenant Henry is sent off to the action at Caporetto which resulted in a total and humiliating defeat for the Italians.

Defeat, like death, is that which halts progress along the moving current of events. The Caporetto defeat is, however, a collective, not a personal one. In the confusion of the resulting rout, the lieutenant, threatened with execution as a traitor, manages to desert and join Catherine. He has escaped the collective plight and is once more united with his love. Together, in scenes as memorable as the ones Hemingway gives us of Caporetto, Catherine and Henry — having got wind that he is to be arrested as a deserter — escape to Switzerland by rowboat across the lake. In this significant crossing they leave behind them the collective conflict and the possible fate of imprisonment; they cross over to peace, to freedom to live a private life together, and to a birthplace for the child Catherine bears. They start life like another Adam, another Eve, in an ideal condition of union in a Paradise of neutrality, among the purity of Swiss snows, with no concern beyond the bringing to successful birth of Catherine's child.

Yet, as every novel-reader knows, the child — a boy — dies at birth. Catherine, too, does not survive an agony of labor, in which we hear a dark echo of that Indian birth so long ago. When Lieutenant Henry walks back from the hospital to the hotel in that famous rain, he is a man totally alone. He has abdicated from man's collective struggle. His love is dead. The child that might have united his male nature with her female, feeling one is dead. He represents the lone, individual male principle, or conscious ego.

From now on Hemingway's heroes will never be the same. From now on, though there will be no lack of women or sex in his novels, the emphasis will be on a man fighting, not to be with his love, not in the common struggle, but against powers that threaten to overwhelm him, represented by bulls, by big game, and by the sea.

We have reached a point where we may view the Hemingway hero as one who, having quit the collective struggle of mankind, has internalized the conflict so that he is at war with whatever it is bulls and lions, gamefish and the ocean represent. A clue to the identity of this opponent, which from now on will occupy so much of the stage in Hemingway's novels, is perhaps to be found in the story "The Short Happy Life of Francis Macomber."

A rich American, Macomber, and his beautiful, unloving wife have gone big-game hunting in Africa with a British white hunter to guide them, Robert Wilson. Macomber runs from his first lion, and his act of cowardice causes the wife, who is hard, unrelenting, demanding, and pitiless, to treat him with utmost contempt and deliberately go to bed with Wilson. Wilson too regards Macomber as a bloody coward, and cowardice is shown as unforgivable. "Wilson suddenly felt as if he had opened the wrong door in a hotel and seen something shameful." Not fear — "A Somali proverb says a brave man is always frightened three times by a lion; when he first sees his track, when he first hears him roar, and when he first confronts him" — but cowardice. The morning after Macomber's wife cuckolds him, they all go hunting after buffalo, as dangerous a quarry as lion. In his anger at his wife, Macomber makes an unexpected conquest of fear which is shown through Wilson's eyes. "Damned if this isn't a strange one, he thought. Yesterday he's scared sick and today he's a ruddy fire-eater. Look at the beggar now! It's that some of them stay little boys so long. The great American boy-men. Damned strange people. But he liked this Macomber now. [His courage] probably meant the end of cuckoldry, too.

Damned good thing. Beggar had probably been afraid all his life. Don't know what started it. But over now. Wilson had seen it, in the war, work the same way. More of a change than any loss of virginity. Fear gone like an operation. Something else grew in its place. Main thing a man had. Made him into a man. Women knew it too. No bloody fear." Sure enough, Mrs. Macomber realizes that her husband has changed, as they wait in the car to go in after the wounded buffalo. " 'You've gotten brave awfully suddenly,' she said contemptuously"; but her contempt was not secure.

Wilson and Macomber go into the brush after the buffalo they have wounded. It rushes out, straight at Macomber. Wilson shoots. Macomber too shoots at the oncoming wicked little pig eyes, and an instant later "felt a sudden white-hot, blinding flash explode within his head, and that was all he ever felt." Mrs. Macomber, back in the car, has shot at the attacking buffalo and hit her husband. She who was so contemptuous of him now weeps hysterically. But Wilson, her lover, is as tough with her as ever she was with Macomber. "Why didn't you poison him?" he remarks. "That's what they do in England." "Stop it!" the woman cries. "I'm through now," Wilson says. "I was a little angry. I'd begun to like your husband." "Oh, please stop it!" she implores. "Please, please stop it!" "That's better," Wilson says. "Please is much better. Now I'll stop."

The reader has learned much. Not only about what is going to be expected of the new Hemingway hero, but what the new Hemingway woman is going to be like. She is going to be, with one exception, nobody's face-to-face, equal love. She is, in part, Woman the Terrible, for we are left in no doubt that what Francis Macomber was really afraid of — that something Wilson wondered about in Macomber's little-boyhood that had started his fear — is the power of woman, the figure symbolized by that Terrible Mother who has the power at once to create and to destroy. Mrs. Macomber possessed all the power until her husband summoned anger enough at her to fight the wild beast; the beast which he formerly funked, the beast we may equate with instinct. Macomber conquers fear through courage, but in the encounter with instinct, is killed. The story says, "Mrs. Macomber, in the car, had shot at the buffalo," but Wilson asks her, "Why didn't you poison him?" and the reader is left in no doubt whatsoever that the woman was, consciously or unconsciously, destroying the man she had possessed so long in the precise moment that he was about to escape from her power. But through his courage, Macomber still took the power away from his wife, who is now reduced to a status where she must beg for good treatment.

This status will be the opposite aspect of the new Hemingway woman — woman the docile, the inferior. She is the tractable Maria of *For Whom the Bell Tolls* — who, for all that she is beautiful and passionate, simple and honest, is an ignorant peasant; Robert Jordan speaks to her as if she were a child. She is the almost halfwittedly submissive Renata of *Across the River and into the Trees,* whom Colonel Cantwell, her elderly, courage-obsessed lover, calls Daughter. The split which we have been pursuing through some of Hemingway's pages may be pinned down nowhere more definitely than in this division of the feminine principle of feeling into two: the fearsome mother-figure — sometimes also beneficent, as in

Pilar of *For Whom the Bell Tolls* — and the immature daughter. Instead of in woman, it seems to me, the hero only tries to meet his match in the shape of these wild beasts, these elemental forces he must battle — recalling the ancient equation between sex and fighting, between the moment of consummation and the moment of death. "The wars are naked that we make tonight." We might call these forces that the Hemingway hero battles Fate; but what is Fate? To quote a psychoanalytical writer, "What we now designate as the collective unconscious was in antiquity conceived of as Fate."

The unconscious is always compensatory to the conscious ego. Hence, to a man, the unconscious possesses a feminine aspect; and indeed the unconscious, as matrix of consciousness, is in an undeniably maternal relation to any individual. We may thus expand an earlier statement to say that the Hemingway hero has internalized the conflict, so that he is at war with the unconscious, feminine forces within him that threaten to overwhelm him. The split is between him and another part of himself; and we have seen, in "The Short Happy Life of Francis Macomber," that we are meant to take the struggle to overcome fear and achieve courage as tantamount to the growing out of little-boyhood, leaving mother, and becoming a man that all men must accomplish.

We have traced, though briefly and glancingly, a series of choices by which the boy turned away from mother, rejected his feminine side, and at last, with the death of his true love, became a man who stands alone against Fate. We have seen that this Fate is terrible only because he is cut off from it; the real problem resides in the abyss that exists between them, the split; or, to put it otherwise, in the hero's not being at one with himself. We have earlier observed that in a sense the split can be said not to exist; since it is a state of not-being that lies between existing opposites. It is comparable to the gap between man's conscious life and that state of Eden he once knew but evicted himself from in growing up, by tasting the fruit of the knowledge of good and evil, or, as we phrased it earlier in a definition of morality, the distinction between good and evil. Into this abyss, as in the case of Francis Macomber, can come what the white hunter Wilson called the something else, that grows in the place of fear when a boy becomes a man. Main thing a man has, Wilson observes. Makes him into a man.

The later work of Hemingway constitutes a literature of courage, if it is courage and not confidence that is the main thing a man has. Anyone who wants to learn what, at least on paper, courage is like, should turn to Hemingway. Or to learn what courage is not. "Cowardice," Hemingway observes, "is almost always a lack of ability to suspend the functioning of the imagination. Learning to suspend your imagination and live completely in the very second of the present, with no before and no after, is the greatest gift a soldier can acquire." In other words, he is saying that courage deals with reality; cowardice, with the fancied. In all of this later work Hemingway is writing about courage, *not* toward Tillich's existential anxiety of non-being, but toward at least fictionally real and fearful forces — bulls, lions, battle, gangsters, buffalo, the sea. Hemingway's courage was never the courage to be, but to do.

In the body of his work Hemingway demonstrates that courage is an individual solution to the collective dilemma; a healer of the wound, a bridge across the split. In place of the chasm, courage rushes in with a relationship; for courage is both toward the object feared and in spite of the fear. Yet when we return to where we started in this search for meanings, to *The Sun Also Rises,* which is about the state of the Hemingway hero *following* the First World War, we find that the problem is still unsolved. Jake is a grown man, alone, out in the world of Paris. But when he meets Brett, that exception who is shown not as mother-figure nor daughter-type, but as Jake's equal, then the wound he sustained in the war (that wound by which he too signed a separate peace that lets him out of the collective plight) renders him unable to possess her; to be united with her. It is represented as being a wound that in no way interferes with Jake's life as a man alone, only with his relation to the woman he wants and who wants him, and who is his co-equal. In this, he is different from other men. He has his wound (the artist's wound?) instead of his love. Because Jake cannot take her, Brett has to scatter herself, and in the end she takes on, as Carlos Baker points out, a definitely sinister quality. Courage, it appears, though essential, is not enough, for the frustration of union between man and woman is still there.

We have hunted for the meaning of the wound, for the meaning of the war, and for an idea about how such wounds are to be healed. There remains, in the police-court reenactment of the central problem in Hemingway's work which *The Sun Also Rises* constitutes, the riddle of the scene's setting; that is to say, the riddle of the meaning of expatriatism. Everything we have said about the split, in other realms, seems to me to be true of expatriatism also, and to be summed up in these lines I quoted earlier: "As cruel a knife/severs my living from my life." The expatriate's *living* goes on in foreign lands; among the strange, the picturesque, the unconventional. His *life*, the core of his being, is where his home is, whether he likes it to be so or not. The first few years of all our lives constitute a sort of core to the rest, fundamentally determining it. The first few years of the Hemingway hero, in the person of Nick, took place in the American West, where the wound began. It is a setting deep into which, in "Big Two-Hearted River," the grown-up Nick did not choose to press on. Instead, rejecting mother-country, heart-land, he prefers, in "Cross Country Snow," an expatriate way of living.

The Hemingway hero's view of the lands on either side of the Atlantic, which we may suspect represent the lands on either side of his inner division, can be learned from the images these two short stories present. In "Big Two-Hearted River," Nick blocks himself from further progress in fishing over home territory, when he thinks of the terrible marsh where "fishing would be tragic." In "Cross Country Snow," he enjoys the sensation, as of flying, on skis over the snow-fields of Switzerland, and says of the sport here, "[Life] isn't worth while if you can't." What is so tragic about fishing in a marsh, and why is skiing so desperately important? I can think of no stronger symbols than those Hemingway has chosen, to convey the opposites of depth and surface. In choosing expatriatism, the hero chooses to live on the surface, skimmingly, hedonistically; in the touching-smelling-seeing-hearing to which he returns after the thought of the marsh defeats him, and by which means the Hemingway hero will in future operate. This surface, snowy world carries connotations of ego awareness, of the future; of action, cleanliness, brightness, outwardness, the height of mountains as well as the sterility of snow. The deep marsh stands for many other things resident in the depths (that is, the unconscious): emotion, tragedy, the danger of being trapped or lost, profundity, inwardness, a backward reaching to the original maternal source, the past; as well as the very fertility of the deep, foul swampiness. The marsh and what it represents is what the Hemingway hero rejects when he rejects home and turns to expatriatism. It is too much for him; the wound was too deep and too painful from its earliest beginning, the Indian woman's screams were too fearful, the Indian man's suicide came as too much of a subjective shock. The man Nick has grown into cannot enter the marsh and fish in it; he can only fight it and all it means from the mountains on the other side of the ocean.

The paragraph that precedes "Cross Country Snow," the expatriate story, concerns a bull-fighter's art in killing a bull, and also his courage. Hemingway's preoccupation with the many arts of sport and killing, of which he writes so brilliantly and so often, seems to me to suggest a preoccupation with art itself, of whatever kind (even that of writing, although Hemingway is far too experienced an artist to write much about writers). Art is what courage needs and summons as a technique for meeting and defeating (or being defeated by) the bulls, the lions, the buffalo, the sea, whose meaning we know. In the world of art, it is possible for the flow of the river of life, that is to say of growth, to go on for a long time after it has been blocked in actual life.

Man's courage to free himself from the collective plight, and to battle alone and consciously against destiny, is certainly one of his major achievements. But we have seen that this battle may not prove to be a completely successful healing of the wound, or a bridge across the chasm, or a reconciliation of the opposites. Nowhere in Hemingway's work will the reader find the hero united with his equal female, or feeling, side. Nowhere will the lion, whose image appears so often in Hemingway's stories and novels, lie down with any lamb. Nowhere will the hero choose, not either or, but either *and* or. The wound, though art and courage battle above it, is still open. The Hemingway hero has not come to terms with woman, with home, or with his life.

One of the several reasons why Hemingway was a great writer is that he kept growing. As long as he lived he continued to surprise us, as when he followed his novel *Across the River and into the Trees,* in which the cult of courage was carried to ridiculous extremes, by the calm wisdom of *The Old Man and the Sea.* One of the several reasons why we can say Hemingway's work had universality is that in it the distinction between good and evil in important human experience is never asserted, only adumbrated; suggested. We could thus add another element to our earlier definition and say: In what is universal fiction there can be no fixed absolutes, no pat solutions. Both in real life and in art the truth is not one thing, but is, perhaps, such a relationship as a paradox contains.

In *The Old Man and the Sea,* the hero is an old fisherman who fights an almost superhuman battle of sheer courage, all alone at sea, against a monstrous fish, and at length wins, only in the end to be defeated by the sharks who eat his catch away to the skeleton while he tows it home. The other character in this prophetic short novel is a boy who loves the old man, and has learned from him everything he knows about the art of fishing. He is a young male figure who is represented as still growing and not, like the old man, at the end of life. At the novel's close the old man, exhausted from his heroic struggle, has fallen asleep and is dreaming about the lions — those lions that everywhere in Hemingway have been equated with courage. The young boy sits besides him, watching him sleep. As the reader closes the book, he may well sorrow for the defeat and death of the old man, while he observes that, even at the end, a boy — the essence of something new — was not far away from where he was; was ready to take over.

SEVEN

The Short Story: Idea and Meaning

IT SEEMS to me that the questions asked by students of the short story, oftenest and most urgently, concern two things. One is how to get ideas for short stories, and the other is how to make the short story hang together.

Now in this book, as I have said before and expect to say again, we are looking at many sorts of writing, less academically, less as literary critics, less from outside, than from the inside, somewhat subjectively, and from the point of view of How do you do it, and how does it feel to do it? Yet it remains true that all books, lectures, literary clinics, and even individual discussions with students have to be conducted analytically. My own view of the structure of the short story, for instance, breaks it down into three stages of composition. First the coming upon the idea for the short story (or its coming upon the writer), together with the gradual, emerging awareness of what it is the idea means, what it is trying to convey. The second step is finding the proper form to contain the idea — the shape, so to speak, of the story, into which idea together with meaning may properly be put. A third stage represents the phase of using technical means — a bagful of tricks — in order to expose the idea, within its form, to public view, so that it may be taken for what it is and not for something else. These include such means as beginnings, writing in scenes, understanding the motives of characters, exploiting the balance of forces that creates the tension of the story, using transition passages as a way of getting, with the maximum effect and value, from one scene to another. Techniques like these are in essence concerned with communication, with getting readers to see what it is hoped they *will* see; sometimes even with getting them to see the story at all.

A good idea, clothed in its appropriate form, can still be so inadequately communicated that a reader is baffled, unable to reach the communication. I remember reading an anthology of four long short stories, one of which had a very interesting idea, put quite properly into novella form. But it was told with incredible clumsiness. In it characters conversed in phrases such as people have never used since the world begun. Everyone's motives were explained in long, earnest detail. The story did have a sort of integrity: an idea with an important meaning, honestly presented. Even so, when I finished it I felt as though I had been working on the railway, and fell with inner cries of relief into the arms of the volume's next story — not nearly so honest a one but told with technical skill by a born writer.

The first of these three stages, that of getting the idea and an inkling of what it means to you, would correspond to the first of the two questions students most often ask, the one about how you get short story ideas. But before I say any more about it, let me hang out the red flag of warning for anyone who has any idea of writing: Don't let me, don't let anybody, ever, give you the false conception that a short story is written in stages. As I said earlier, the method of any lecture or essay on writing has to be reductive; the short story (or whatever) is taken apart to see what makes it tick. Then it is, presumably, put together again and all should be able to roll on merrily from there. But apparently that is not always what happens. It seems to be all too possible for writers, even fairly experienced writers, to think of the short story (or whatever) not as a self-contained entity but as a lot of separate parts. I remember a charming man at a lecture of mine who raised his hand in the question period and asked, "Do you simply write the basic story first, and then put the symbolism in?"

This leads straight back to the second of those most-often-put questions, the one about how to make a short story hang together. Obviously one answer would be *not* to think about it as though it were a jigsaw puzzle lying on a table, which, if you pick it up, will drop apart. I would like to use the Toynbeean image of withdrawal and return to illustrate the initial getting of ideas for short stories, or as far as that goes, ideas for any fiction. The writer out in the world, out in his life, finds his consciousness impinged upon by something so startling that he cannot quickly adapt to it or assimilate it, but must — if he is a writer — withdraw to consider what struck him; that strange fury, beauty, or despair. From it, let us hope, an idea for a story emerges. After the writer has explored its meaning to him, he begins wondering what its meaning might be to other people. At that point he can begin to emerge, to return, conveyed on wings of the need to communicate. I might add that, like a wise virgin, the writer needs to keep himself in readiness for that moment when consciousness is impinged upon. In that moment when two things meet, himself and something outside of himself, their meeting explodes into a third thing, a story. If the writer does not keep listening for ideas he might easily take this moment of impingement for something unpleasant, and shrink from it. As Elizabeth Bowen says, "There is not so much a search as a state of open susceptibility."

But a short story does not consist of withdrawal and return any more than it does of idea and meaning, or of form, or of technical means of communication. A short story is nothing of the sort. It is, or ought to be, an impenetrably integrated whole. Moreover, the various stages of its composition which I have mentioned occur not in sequence or separately but all at the same time. For instance, it is impossible for a writer to get an idea for a story without at the same time getting an inkling of the form it will eventually be cast in. He cannot visualize his story in its form without at the same time glimpsing some of the technical illusions he will need to convey the thing he sees. It is only for purposes of simplification, and because one can't talk about three things at once, that I am going to speak as though the writing of the short story takes place in stages.

Once I spoke at a writer's conference in Pittsburgh in company with another writer, a man. In one of the sessions he discussed J. D. Salinger's "For Esmé — with Love and Squalor." A young woman in the audience kept raising her hand, and each time the speaker would nod to her and she would ask, about whatever point he had been mentioning, "Is that plot?" or "Is that characterization?" Each time my colleague would reply, "Not entirely." Finally the young woman raised her hand for about the fifth time and asked, "Which is plot and which is characterization?" He exploded, saying, "I haven't the faintest idea." I fear the young woman may have gone away and told her friends, "Mr. S—— doesn't know the difference between plot and characterization." He hadn't the faintest idea, not because he was incapable of analysis, but because he wouldn't allow himself to think in the divisive terms by which a short story can be dissected and put away into little tin boxes, like minerals.

It really is a bad habit for a writer, one that will do him harm, to keep thinking of a story of any kind in terms of its separate elements. I think it is as valuable a lesson as any the writer can learn, to practice thinking about a story in his mind as a whole — fluid, flexible, reworkable at any moment. I don't mean that he should be uncritical toward it; he should be mercilessly critical, impossible to please. But he should try to keep his hands on the whole thing at once, as though it were a lump of clay that a sculptor keeps wet to render it workable. Writing is much harder to keep all in one piece than a lump of clay, because literature, unlike sculpture, is made up of dozens of phantasies, like so many shuttlecocks made of feathers, that bob all around. Somehow the writer must manage to keep the whole dancing thing accessible to his mind at the same time until he gets his overall effect.

When I say the writer should be impossible to please I mean, of course, that he must edit himself. It is interesting how many of the human traits least desirable in real life seem to come in very handy — are in fact indispensable — in writing. Self-doubt — self-criticism — obsession with the idea of perfection — in life one would view these qualities askance, but they are just grand for being a writer with. The writer should doubt his own work in relation to its potential readers, not assume that what seems a fascinating witticism to him will strike his reader as anything but pretentious. He should be critical of everything that seems to him most delightful in his style. He should excise what he most admires, because he wouldn't thus admire it if he weren't, by so doing, in a sense protecting it from criticism. He should not have faith in his story's being good just because he likes it. An editor once said to me, of a writer who contributes to his magazine, "The trouble with K—— is, he thinks every idea that comes into his head is a good one just because it's his head it came into." The same editor, on another occasion, observed dreamily, "The best writing seems to be the product of self-doubt."

Furthermore, in real life it is very far from wise to project one's self-doubts on to other people — imagining, for example, that one's husband is disdainful of one's cooking ability, when in actual fact that poor man's silence only means he is leaving well enough alone. Yet in writing fiction it will do the writer no harm at all to imagine what people might say of his attempted wit, his big emotional scene, his subtle ending. Of course it will only be himself who is saying all those mocking, sarcastic things, but readers can be mocking and sarcastic too, and it is as well to be prepared for them. Again, in real life it is childish — immature is the jargon word — to imagine things differently from what in fact they are, to woolgather, daydream, fail to accept reality. But what else is fiction but woolgathering and daydreaming? If it is anything at all, it is a refusal to accept the way things are and an effort to create them as if they had been otherwise.

I would say that a good overall attitude for the writer to adopt to his work is, first, a large, inclusive, forbearing love of it, with all the mistakes he will certainly make; enough love to make him stick with it through thick and thin. And second, a nasty, picky, fault-finding dissatisfaction with all the work's details. He should be toward his work a combination of cherishing mother and severest critic. If he ever does get the work finished and published, it will be quite time enough for leaning back to wonder at what he hath wrought.

Where does that first germ of an idea for a story come from? Readers as well as writers seem fascinated by the question. Readers often ask a writer where he gets his ideas, much as people back in Prohibition would ask who a friend's bootlegger was. Yet if the writer replies truthfully and says, perhaps, that he gets them from looking out of the window, readers seem dissatisfied. "I mean, what do you get your ideas *from*," they repeat; perhaps the writer didn't hear them right the first time. "You must have great powers of observation."

Much is said in lay circles about the powers of observation writers have, and much, too, of their perfidy in using as the basis of their work some story told in confidence, or human tragedy heartlessly reported. People have often said to me, "I suppose you carry a notebook everywhere with you." Other people, shown my study at home, look about and finally inquire for the file-cases in which I am supposed to keep my index of character descriptions. But the actual fact is that observation plays little part in the birth of story ideas. Or rather, the sort of reportorial observation which such people as these have in mind probably took place long, long before the idea itself was born. If it is a good idea, and the writer's own, the observation has to have been assimilated to such a point that it is no longer recognizable as observation.

Story ideas are, as I have suggested, the result of a psychic marriage between outer reality and inner phantasy. Something in life strikes the writer, the nature of which he is ignorant about, and phantasy rushes in to explain his experience. As Elizabeth Bowen puts it, "The writer, unlike his non-writing friend, seldom observes deliberately. He sees what he did not intend to see; he remembers what does not seem wholly possible. His is the roving eye. By that eye is his subject found. The glance, at first only vaguely caught, goes on to concentrate, deepen; becomes the vision. Just what *has* he seen, and why should it mean so much? The one face standing out of the crowd, the figure in the distance crossing the street, the glare or shade significant on a building, the episode playing out at the next table, the image springing out of a phrase of talk, the disproportionate impact of some one line of poetry — why should this or that be of such importance as to bring all else to a momentous stop? Fate has worked, as in a falling in love."

And what is Fate, that works in these irrational ways its wonders to perform? As we saw in an earlier section, "What we now designate as the collective unconscious was in antiquity conceived of as Fate." The unconscious — that repository of emotion, instinct, and memory underlying consciousness and at times seeming to impinge upon it — sends up those phantasy explanations for the unknown that result in story ideas. It is a subtle blend. Too much reality and not enough phantasy renders a sterile plot. Too much imagination and too little of the real world may end up in awful little tales I can only call puckish. In any case, imagination is the matrix of the story idea;

and what is needed if the story is to be given birth is a feeling for phantasy, a feeling for imagining — feeling for it, rather than suspicion of it.

The odium in which daydreaming is held in our culture is a quite understandable antipathy. Imagining is certainly at the root of many of our most vicious habits — malicious gossip, unrealistic fears, unfounded self-importance. Let us consider a couple of daydreams, so that we may observe how aggressive and destructive they may be. First, a young married woman in a small town is made so wretched by the memories of past triumphs in New York that she comes to loathe everyone around her, fancies them all jealous of her beauty and critical of her behavior, wastes her substance on longings for the vanished past, feels superior to her quiet, devoted husband because he is satisfied with this boring community; and hence is a ready subject for an extra-marital affair.

Second, another young, but unmarried, woman in a small town gets her feelings hurt when an out-of-town young man, considered a great catch, doesn't dance with her at a party in a neighbor's house. She builds up her grievance into a dislike for him bordering on hatred, a hatred so unreasonable that when she hears the young man slandered she at once accepts the libel as true. She is so unable to see any good at all in him that she makes of him a sort of ogre, incapable of human decency, and comes close to missing out on the marital intentions which he in fact entertains toward her.

Both these young women built up vain constructions out of sheer phantasy. The first of the two stories really happened recently, in a town which I was visiting, and ended in divorce. The second constitutes the plot of *Pride and Prejudice*. My point is that in ordinary life everyone exercises amazing powers of imagination; I am continually struck by the tall tales fabricated in the course of an afternoon's gossip among ladies. It will be obvious how much more suitable a place fiction is for their employ than life.

Due, perhaps, to the horror engendered in us since child-hood of exaggeration, distortion, and lying, most of us have not developed our imaginations to the point where they can be used consciously — as flexible, sensitive, and fertile. Instead we tend to gossip, under the impression that we are discussing matters of actual knowledge instead of Frost's "our guessing at each other." Most people, when they imagine consciously, are feeble, timid, and sterile at it. Some children, even, hardly imagine at all. This inability is strikingly expressed by the doubt people display in the very existence of imagination. And I am often impressed by the exceedingly poor grasp many people have of the difference between fiction and reality.

The psychoanalysts may be concerned when patients substitute phantasy for reality, but I am concerned when readers cannot let go of the notion that a story, because written in the first person, actually happened to the author. Such confusion of fact and fancy can be drastically exhibited when the aficionados of TV soap operas send real wedding presents, costing real money, to a soap-opera bride, and then, not two months later, can invest in real layettes for her impending soap-opera confinement. It is all to be compared with the confusion felt by my son — aged, however, only six at the time — when he had the privilege of viewing the real Roy Rogers on the street of our town, and then came home to hear Roy Rogers's voice issuing from a radio broadcast from Hollywood. It upset him terribly.

But imagination can be cultivated. To use imagination efficiently means to be able to let go, temporarily, of the sense of outer reality. The late John Van Druten once wrote, "I have found that writing problems are easiest for me when I am driving a car. I think this is because I can forget my body and my sense of myself. That 'I' is the important word. It is the word that must be forgotten, and forgotten not deliberately but involuntarily, in the absorption of the task. I have a sense of turning to something outside myself. Yet I know, too, that what I am listening to comes from within me, although I cannot hear it unless I forget that fact. In the end I suppose I mean no more by this than lies in the words, 'Of myself can I do nothing.' "

For an example of the genesis of a story idea I will venture to describe a story of my own, principally because I remember how it began. In literary criticism one has to guess at beginnings, conjecture associations, piece together the little that can be known. In the case of this story, "A Summer's Long Dream," I was spending the summer in an old stone house beside the sea. It was in a mere cluster of summer houses — not a resort at all. Every day as I washed the lunch dishes I used to see, crawling down the road like black beetles, two old ladies who were spending the summer in a neighboring house, cared for by their daughter and niece — a brilliant, tense young woman. I never said more to either of them than to pass the time of day. It was their black-beetle aspect that got me.

I usually rather enjoy washing dishes. But one day when I was in a hurry I thought how unpleasant it is to have to do housework when you want to be doing something else, and then I had the corollary thought that a great many people spend their entire adult lives doing almost entirely what they don't want to. This — the vision of the lady beetles and the thought of the young woman's drudgery and look of repression — was all the story idea amounted to, but perhaps I should add that I myself was in rather a bad temper that summer from quite other causes than those which I invented for the young woman in my story to be frustrated by. In any case, the story continued to rise, as stories do, in my mind as I woke up in the mornings, each day with some new addition, as though it were a log of driftwood that I kept pushing down into the sea only to have it rise again with more seaweed, more barnacles encrusted on it. Some writers achieve the incremental process, by which a story attracts to itself what belongs in it, by continual rewriting; the basic idea becomes enlarged with each revision. Other writers, I one of them, find the story grows outside of consciousness. Work is done on the story with the conscious mind and then it is pushed down for a day or several days or more, after perhaps a few notes have been taken to capture the story's development. When it next rises into consciousness it always seems to have changed and to have added new elements. The big risk is in deciding when to begin writing; although here, too, the most important thing is to keep the idea as whole as possible in one's mind: flexible, not pinned down irrevocably, until the idea can be gradually manipulated into its final form in words.

In the end "A Summer's Long Dream" turned out to be about a woman of thirty-nine who is in a sort of bondage to her mother and her aunt. The bondage is the duty she feels she owes them because they are old and pitiful, and it is based on the compulsions of her bringing-up to be unselfish, to be kind, to be always polite. The bondage, thus, is to the past. The reader comes upon Penelope sitting on the moldering terrace of a huge seashore house at a decaying summer resort, once fashionable. The house has been left to her and her relatives to live in for the month of August, by the will of a rich aunt. Thereafter it is to be sold at auction. The rich dead aunt had once entertained Penelope and her mother here, long ago, when Penelope was a little girl and when the resort was still smart. But now times have changed.

Before Penelope left their home in West Virginia, where she works as a judge's secretary, she had pled with her mother to bring along a maid, so that they could all be free to enjoy a month of leisure. But both old ladies had cried out at the expense of such a thing, and insisted they would all pitch in together and the work would be done with ease. But in the end, just as she had foreseen, it has fallen to Penelope's lot to do, and when the reader discovers her she is inwardly railing against the old tyrants; longing for freedom and dreaming of how wonderful it would be if she were out sailing in one of the white-sailed craft she sees on the ocean, in company with people her own age, instead of spending her holiday slaving in this vast, effort-consuming mansion. Sailing seems to sum up for her the liberty she wants.

A memory comes to her of that long-ago visit when she was a child and free of responsibility — although, since she had never learned to swim, her mother had not allowed her to go out in a boat then. She remembers overhearing her mother, during that earlier visit, discussing her with their hostess, the late Cousin Carrie. She heard them agree that Penelope was a selfish child, and Penelope, eavesdropping, had felt wounded and guilty. Back now, in the present, she reflects bitterly that it is really her elders who are selfish; it is they who are enjoying life without consideration for her. *She* is the one who is losing out on everything, she thinks, as she looks yearningly out where another lovely white sailboat has appeared in the pale blue view. She is filled with fury at how they have exploited her — a fury she often feels and can never express, because the words that flood her mind are too violent — too impolite — to be said to old ladies.

At this point in her reflections the old ladies return from one of the walks they are always taking. They have run into a resident of the resort, who has asked them all to a garden party. They crow over Penelope, who had been so sure that there was no social life at all here any more. "You see, it isn't necessary always to be so gloomy," her mother says. Later they go to the party. Penelope shepherds the old ladies, who brush her off as soon as they get there and proceed to have a splendid time. As Penelope stands alone, looking at a bed of sweet williams in the garden, a pleasant man comes up and makes conversation, in the course of which he asks her to go sailing with him. "Oh, no," she replies instantly. "I'm afraid I couldn't. You see, I can't swim."

As the story ends, the three women are walking slowly home after the party in the dusk, to that huge old ruined house which is a sort of monument to Cousin Carrie, her life and times. They can hear the ocean beyond the sea wall swinging back and forth, against the rocks forever.

This story was a combination of the bare idea I got as I stood washing dishes, together with what I gradually began to grasp as some of the meanings of the idea — as that the sailboat acted as an embodiment to Penelope of the freedom she hadn't won; as that bondage always seems to be from without and always is from within. If the story had not meant a lot to me I could not have summoned the energy to write it. But it did mean a very great deal to me. It is still coming to mean more different things to me all the time.

People who aren't writers love to offer plots to writers. "Here," they will say. "Here is an anecdote I heard the other day at a cocktail party. It'll amaze you! You'll be able to make a wonderful story out of it." I have developed a built-in cringe for the moments when someone offers me a story, because I have never been able to make use of the stories that are offered to me; anyway, not so far. They are not my stories. Although they are often funny or fantastic or dramatic stories, the fact that they do not mean anything private to me keeps me from summoning the vital energy, and by that I don't mean the physical energy, to write them. The energy and the enthusiasm. They literally leave me cold.

I think this is a general experience among writers. If somebody else's anecdote does ever become a story of one's own, I think it is because chords in the anecdote strike echoes in one's own experience. Not literal echoes, but echoes of meaning. If a story about East Africa happened to strike an echo of private meaning in me, I suspect that although I have never been to East Africa I might be more able to write it than one about, say, Cambridge, Massachusetts, where I have been so often. This shows one more facet of how a story has to be kept a whole in one's mind if it is ever to come to life. The story has got to have its private meaning to the author, or it is not whole. For idea is only the outside of any story, and meaning is its inner side.

One often hears the proposition advanced that our world has become meaningless. This seems to me poppycock. Nothing can be meaningless. If writers are not involved in life enough, or are in too much of a hurry, or are too egotistical, or if they are perhaps — which would be understandable — too afraid of life to find meanings in the world of today, that doesn't mean that there aren't any meanings. But I think I had better define what I mean by meaning; or perhaps I should say define what meaning, in fiction, is not.

It is not, or I do not mean that it is, a moral. Joyce Cary once said, "If it is dangerous to say that a story has a moral, let us call it a meaning. What, then, does *Tristram Shandy* mean? To read it is an event and remains a memory, like a meeting of which one says 'It meant a lot to me.'" Here I will be talking about meaning in the sense usually expressed by the word *value*. I am unable to see the point of anyone's writing a story that carries no value to him (or therefore to anyone else). A short story should be an event that means something; that reveals something; that matters. This is not to say a short story should merely build up and establish a point. I heard a writer say once that the fascinating thing about Eudora Welty's work is the manner in which she fractures meaning. I take this to mean that in a short story it is as important and exciting to see meaning taken apart and dissolved as it is to see meaning set up. In either case meaning has to be there. Meaning cannot be shown overtly; meaning is the other side, the hind side, of the coin of idea, or plot. Meaning is the power behind the idea, the force strong enough to impel the writer, whether he is yet aware of his meaning or not, to take the trouble and pains to write the story. It is what makes the reader read it. It is what makes the story matter.

Read William Faulkner's "A Rose for Emily." It tells the story of an old, eccentric recluse. Does it not also tell the inexpressible, the intricate and subtle story of pride in the postbellum South? Read Salinger's "For Esmé — with Love and Squalor." It seems to be a brilliant study of a shell-shocked soldier's feeling for a beguiling little girl. Salinger might not have been impelled to write this story, however, if it had not also been about some private suffering and horror, and about the nature of love. One can read many of Hemingway's stories as evocations of an outdoor life — hunting, fishing, and skiing. But why are they so different from all other sports stories, unless it is because, as Edmund Wilson puts it, "we are made to feel, behind the appetite for the physical world, the tragedy or the falsity of a moral relation. We may find in Hemingway — the clairvoyant's crystal of a polished, incomparable art — the image of the common oppression."

What I mean by meaning, what I look for in a short story, is the reverberation of significance beyond the matters immediately under observation. I want to be able to look up from the end of a story and then, slowly, as what I have read sifts down, to have the flower of relevance open for me. Some writers that pass for very good today don't seem to me to have left room in their brilliant surfaces for any meaning to rise. When the bell of their story has stopped ringing, that is the end. There isn't any reverberation. When a story is really good and really has meaning, it is like a glass that, struck, gives out a clear ringing that you can hear awakened in still other glasses, as you go about the day's work; that keeps sending that rung note farther and deeper and fainter down into consciousness.

The editor of a magazine that publishes short stories once wrote me, "Unless the writer's mind is on good working terms with his imagination, then surface itself takes on depth — is the only depth there is. If a writer is not sure of what he means, he usually swings out on some ornament, and, turning in mid-air, grasps at another ornament and then steps down onto a little platform with a bow. For some time acrobatics like this have been fashionable. Story in the sense of a furnished room, that you can move into and out of at will — overt story — is always important, because fiction-writers are descended from the professional story-tellers, and not from the prophets. But overt story should always be seated at the hostess's left; truth, point, the sense of life, meaning, on her right."

If a writer is not sure of what he means. I believe that one of the things that can really be learned about writing is to find out, or to try to find out, what one means. Of course one must be spontaneous — or rather, sound spontaneous. Of course one must never spell things out. It is an insult to the reader, as well as a great mistake artistically, to try to tell the reader what meaning he is supposed to find in a story. But one can, privately, in the inner place where the story is hatched, make sure of what it is one does mean.

This is not easy. Often I have had to stop several times before I got to the end of a story and write down, on a separate piece of paper, in a sentence or two, just what it is that I am trying to say, before I can go on. It may be that some writers have a perfectly clear idea of what it is they mean to say in a story, and that it stays the same for them from the first day of composition. But, judging from the short stories I read, I doubt it. I doubt that they always know what they mean, and I doubt that what they mean stays the same for the fifth or the twentieth day of writing that it was for the first. Meaning is always elusive, and it tends to change with the development of the story.

It is immensely important to keep a finger on the pulse of one's developing meaning. What am I trying to say? a writer might ask himself every day during the composition of a short story, and every day make a slightly different reply. But he should always ask. He should not trust the answer to good luck. He should not expect it to come along with the story automatically, like airplane baggage. Like baggage, it is all too likely to get diverted en route. I have read story after story in short story contests that must have started with an excellent idea, which subsequently got fouled up. It may have got lost in the excitement of inventing an effective ending. It may have been mislaid if the writer became fatally interested in the mechanics of his plot, to the exclusion of his characters. Sometimes the author seems to have simply forgotten what it was that seemed to him worth writing a story about when he first got his idea and just gone ahead and finished it, hoping that his lapse of memory would not be detected. But if a writer isn't sure what it is he wants to say in his short story, how can the reader ever be expected to guess?

Of course there are some, we might call them writers, who prefer not to know what they mean. They may even consider it glamorous not to know. My favorite literary story was told me by a friend who, lunching at the Colony in New York, heard from the next table one chic young woman say to another, "My dear, I'm writing a novel. It's the most obscure thing!"

I prefer to stand in the ranks of those who put their trust in clarity. Clarity is not at all an easy thing to achieve. To discern what it is one means, and then to express it with lucidity, is extremely difficult. Furthermore, clarity is not the same thing as obviousness. If one's subject and one's meaning are subtle, then to express them with clarity is, ipso facto, subtle too. It never seems to me a good idea when writers attempt to be subtle about what is obvious, or when they are obscure if it is possible, by whatever toil, to be lucid.

❦

EIGHT

The Short Story: More about Form

AS WE have seen, idea may be called the front of a short story and meaning the back — and let us have no fancy quibbling about what meaning is. Meaning, as we are using it here, means simply the meaning of the idea, both to author and to reader. Idea is what the reader comes on when he scans the story, what he can express when he in turn tries to tell somebody else what the story was about; idea is the outer curve. Meaning is whatever writer and reader feel, what they are moved by, what makes the story important to them; the inward half. Together they make up a whole, and each particular story's whole will have characteristics of its own — a special size and shape, which is that story's inherent form.

There is in print a paperback collection called *A Book of Stories*. I first bought it when traveling, under the impression that it was a collection of distinguished short stories, because, quickly leafing through it in the shop, I noticed one or two short stories I especially admire, and which I wanted to possess in convenient light-weight form. When I got back to my hotel room, however, I found that this collection is something rather different. It is, sure enough, a book of stories. It includes, sure enough, several examples of narrative within the short story form. But it also contains some poems, a letter, excerpts from a journal, several fables and fairy tales, and one of the books of the Bible.

The editor of the collection, Randall Jarrell, included an introduction in which he defines a story. First he gives the dictionary definition — "a narrative, recital, or description of what has occurred; also a fictitious narrative, imaginative tale; also a lie, a falsehood." He adds, "A story, then, can be a wish or a truth, or a wish modified by a truth." He goes on to define a story further as a sort of dream, in that it satisfies wishes. A story is a chain of events. Stories, he says, are always capable of generalization; a story about a dog Kashtanka (I suppose in Chekhov's *Vanka*) is true for all values of dogs and men. He gives another example: the marker that the men at Fort Benning put up over their buried dog, Calculus — "He made better dogs of us all."

Jarrell goes on to say, "When we try to make, out of the stories life gives us, works of art of comparable concision, we almost always put them into verse. . . . A truly representative collection of stories would include many more poems." In further discussing what he chose for inclusion, Jarrell speaks of the severe difficulty of putting together any collection that will represent the protean nature of the story. Proust's *Remembrance of Things Past* is a story; St. Simon's *Memoirs* are a collection of stories; epic poems are stories; *Moby Dick* is a story; *Great Expectations* is a story. But even if one limits oneself to short narratives, he says, there are so many such, of every kind, that a book the size of his cannot even begin to represent them. He regrets too that he has had to leave out all sagas, all ballads, all myths, and has been forced to omit Homer, Plutarch, and Dostoevski.

Now with these definitions of what stories may be I heartily — because the definitions are so heartening — agree. Stories are in everything. One of the really great moments in the life of a writer is that one I have spoken of earlier, when he realizes that far from ever needing fear for a lack of stories to tell, every single thing, every single person, every single situation within his orbit is, potentially, a story.

But once we have got over the excitement of this discovery and accepted that stories may be of innumerable kinds — true or untrue, short or long, epic or epigrammatic — there is still something unsatisfactory about Mr. Jarrell's definitions when we come to discuss, not stories, but the short story, and the form of the short story. I am here discussing the short story. I know what I mean by the short story. My reader knows what he or she means by the words "short story." The chances are that neither reader nor I means for one moment the whole of Proust, or of the Iliad. But our agreement is not merely over a short story's being something short. A story that is short is not necessarily a short story, any more than a story as long as *War and Peace* is. Randall Jarrell has included in his collection of not short stories but stories, the following story from Chuang T'zu. "Lieh Tzu, being on a journey, was eating by the roadside when he saw an old skull. Plucking a blade of grass, he pointed to it and said, 'Only you and I know that there is no such thing as life, and no such thing as death.'"

That is short, it is possibly a story, but I am quite sure it is not what anybody means when he speaks of a short story.

Also included in Jarrell's collection is Robert Frost's "The Witch of Coös." But while this tells an eerie story wonderfully, clearly it is not, at least in form, a short story, but a poem. The Book of Jonah is also included in Jarrell's collection. Now, the Book of Jonah is one of the most exciting and intriguing stories ever told, one which conveys in the telling meanings which even after these thousands of years people have not fully grasped. Is it a short story, or isn't it?

I have described Jarrell's collection of stories at such length only in order to build a springboard from which we may take off into a consideration of what we do mean when we say "the short story." Here again we touch on the importance of meaning. If a would-be writer doesn't know what he means by a short story, I don't see how he can possibly write one, any more than I can see how he could possibly dig a ditch if he didn't know what he meant by one. He might instead keep digging straight down and end up with a well. The collection I have been describing is an excellent one, full of an assortment of good things, but a man from Mars who wanted to become a short story writer might read it and, if he was under the impression that its stories were all short stories, end up by writing a sonnet sequence, or a letter to his fair cousin back in space, and then submitting it for publication at the usual rates as an Atlantic First.

The short story is, to put it in the starkest terms, a form into which some narratives may suitably be put; just as the novel and the epic and the letter are other forms into which other narratives may suitably be put. When we talk about the short story, then, we mean in part a form. As I observed at the beginning, idea and meaning together form a whole, which possesses its own shape or character; this shape is the intrinsic form of the story, which it is the work of the writer to discover.

Once while I was staying at the MacDowell Colony, a writer there read aloud one evening at the library from his recently published volume of short stories. He read two of them. One was what I should indeed call a short story. The other was about a woman who feels, on returning from a trip away alone, that her husband is becoming indifferent to her. He and she then take a trip together to New Hampshire in an effort to come closer through witnessing an ancient folk-dance which they had seen performed on their honeymoon. During the performance a forest fire starts, and the husband goes to help fight it. Later, the couple go away again, and in quite another place encounter a rough type of man who at first frightens the woman, though later she becomes aware that she is attracted by his very roughness. It gradually emerges that the husband has a homosexual disposition. In the end the woman comes to realize that it is really she who has become indifferent to her husband.

All of this took one hour and a half to read aloud, and it is most interesting and revealing, but it did not seem to me to be a short story. Not because it was so long, but because it seemed more like material for a novel. The heroine's mind slowly, slowly changes in the course of the narrative. The husband is revealed as abnormal very, very gradually. The forest fire is dealt with at length, in detail; it almost constitutes a study of the techniques of forest-fire fighting. The country dance, with its origins in the past, is treated exhaustively. The resolution, when at last it does come, is something that has been worked up to — Frank O'Connor's "logical, inescapable flowering of events." Within such a mass of material, the stuff of a short story is, without doubt, concealed; but the story as it was read to us that evening was not, successfully, a short story. What it was I can only guess, since my imagination was never really taken by the idea. But I would guess that it was a novel or at least a novella.

Time, in the short story, is not merely a matter of how long it takes to read the story. Rather, time is, in the short story, condensed; telescoped; manipulated. It is made use of, to serve the story's requirements. The idea of the short story, and the meaning behind the idea, are best displayed to advantage when the narrative can be, so to speak, jelled into one discrete mold, a shape, a design. When this mold has been found, and cunningly used, the short story does not so much flow along as explode, or, shall we say, happen. It should never flow, because it is not moving from one point off in the direction of another point; it is happening all on one point. This point, which is the same thing as the mold, may be a day, or the character of a protagonist; or it may be a house, or a town, or a dream, or a fight. In any case a number of events and characters are being viewed, as O'Connor puts it, from some glowing center of action.

Many novels also center on one character, one event, or one place; but their whole purpose, their rhythm, is different. The novel form does specifically permit the passage of time, characters, and events from one point off in the direction of another point — or to several other points. The short story, while it may involve a number of years, personal destinies, or a combination of many events or destinies, must tie them all in one knot, explode them in one crisis, combine them in a gestalt. When I was very young and trying to teach myself how to write short stories I put down on a piece of paper I still possess — put down in some desperation, I think, as the handwriting looks shaky — "Don't Explain Anything. Don't Preach. Simple, Sensuous, Passionate." and then, underlined, *"Make it All One Thing."*

Faulkner, when at one of his lecture-conferences at the University of Virginia, he was asked why he chose the novel form to write in, said that it was because the novel was the form he could best manipulate, and that he felt himself to be at heart a poet. He suggested that the poem is the form which comes closest to the original impulse of any writer, the form which approaches most nearly to an absolute statement of meaning. The short story, he added, is next nearest to the artist's self, and the novel the farthest away. If this is so, it might explain the impression one receives and should receive that a short story, nearly as much as a poem, is not so much *about* a thing as it is the thing itself. Its meaning is very close to a being. The short story less concerns occurrences than, itself, occurs.

Time in the short story should generally be treated unrealistically. It is an artifice. The other elements in the short story — character, action, mood — must carry the burden of verisimilitude. Time in the short story should possess rather the quality of time as it is experienced in moments of insight, in intuitive flashes, which, when they are over, leave one not knowing whether five seconds or an hour have passed.

We have seen in an earlier section that the short story is like making a decision. The short story can also be said to come upon the reader like what the French call the *coup de foudre* — a thunderclap; like, in the meaning of the idiom, falling in love. It is remarkably like falling in love, rather rashly. What does the reader know of these characters' antecedents? Of where they went to school? He knows only what he sees before him, and that but little. But, also like someone in love, he feels that that is all he needs to know. At least it is the task of the short story writer to make him feel that way. O'Connor calls the short story "lyrical and not epic" — which is again like falling in love.

The novel, with rare exceptions, is not a lyric expression, it is not the song of the lark. It is something slower, steadier, more studied than falling in love; perhaps marriage is its prototype. Instead of giving that lyric cry, it turns soberly to the world, it turns to society, and involves, in almost every case you will find, the relation of the individual to society. There are of course those exceptions; I can think of several. Eudora Welty's *Delta Wedding* prolongs the fresh explosiveness of a short story. Virginia Woolf's *Mrs. Dalloway* takes place within the unities of time, place, and point of view of a short story, together with the mood of one.

The short story, on the other hand, deals with the individual in relation to himself. His problems, his desires, his fears and sorrows are the short story's material, and they exist within a purely personal circle, within himself. Thus we may make another analogy, that the short story form, besides being like a decision, and like a falling in love, is like an individual and can contain what an individual can. The short story bears upon this center of individual concerns, and not outward upon society. Naturally, to this image there are exceptions too. It seemed to me at the time they first came out that Salinger's "Raise High the Roofbeam, Carpenters" and "Zooey" were novel material, treated as a novel would be, and indeed since that time a conviction has grown among his admirers that the Glass stories are intended to some day take their places in a comprehensive novel about the rarefied society of Glasses. Faulkner's short stories about the early days of Yoknapatawpha County have qualities — of pace, for example — of a novel, and it will be observed that they are, after all, studies of pioneer man under primitive conditions, striving to *establish* a society.

It might be interesting to consider a few short stories to discover the crises, the decisions, the individuals on which they focus. Faulkner's "That Evening Sun" is a story about a colored woman in the Deep South, Nancy, pregnant by a white man, working for a white family, who knows that if she goes back to her own cabin her husband, who has been in hiding, will come out of the darkness and cut her throat with his razor. The white family is willing to let her sleep in their house for safety, but she will not. Not that she isn't afraid; she is terrified. She tries to get the white children she cares for to stay in her cabin with her, knowing that while they are there her husband will not come. But the children, through whose eyes the story is seen, get bored with the tales with which she tries to entertain them, and weary of her attempts to pop corn. Their father comes to fetch the children home and advises Nancy to go to some friend's house, since she is so panicky, but she will not. She is paralyzed by fatalism.

The idea of the story seems to me to be built around Nancy's choice of death. Its meaning is everywhere evident in the almost unbearable tension of pity, understanding, and despair for Nancy, a black island in a dominant white sea where such a choice as hers could seem the only one. Together this idea and this meaning have a shape, which form can be called a short story.

Salinger's "For Esmé — with Love and Squalor" is about a soldier in World War II and a little English girl with whom he has a conversation remarkable for its candor and absurdity, just before the D day invasions. The soldier is shell-shocked in the fighting on the Continent, in a dangerous state of depression in his quarters in Bavaria, and close to suicide when he receives a letter from his little friend in England, as candid and absurd as her conversation, sending him as a present her wrist watch, "which you may keep in your possession for the duration of the conflict." The story ends with the soldier's feeling his first normal impulse toward sleep in weeks. In effect he has chosen life. This is the idea of the story, and its meaning seems to me to lie in the judgment on war and war's effects expressed when the soldier copies out a quotation from Dostoevski in the fly-leaf of a book he has found in the house where he is quartered. The former occupant of the house, a Nazi now under arrest, had already written in it: "Dear God, life is hell." What the soldier adds underneath is, "Fathers and teachers, I ponder 'What is hell?' I maintain that it is the suffering of being unable to love." Hate, war, is hell — squalor — and love is life, which the soldier is at last able to choose because of his feeling for Esmé. The story is buried deep in such concentric layers of one individual's suffering and longing that it is inconceivable it could be anything but a short story.

Many short story anthologies include that remarkable work of E. B. White's, "The Door." It probably is a short story. It certainly deals with choice — in fact it is entirely concerned with the difficulties of choice-making. It is about a man deciding to step out of a very ambiguous door. He ends by doing so. Meanwhile, for five pages he reflects upon the problem of making any choice.

Now about those rats, he kept saying to himself. He meant the rats that the Professor had driven crazy by forcing them to deal with problems which were beyond the scope of rats, the insoluble problems. He meant the rats that had been trained to jump at the square card with the circle in the middle and the card (because it was something it wasn't) would give way and let the rat into a place where the food was; but then one day it would be a trick played on the rat, and the card would be changed, and the rat would jump but the card wouldn't give way, and it was an impossible situation (for a rat) and the rat would go insane and into its eyes would come the unspeakably bright imploring look of the frustrated, and after the convulsions were over and the frantic racing around, then the passive stage would set in and the willingness to let anything be done to it, even if it was something else. . . . Nobody can *not* jump. Everybody has to keep jumping at a door (the one with the circle on it), because that is the way everybody is, especially some people. I remember the door with the picture of the girl on it, her arms outstretched in loveliness, her dress (it was the one with the circle on it) uncaught, beginning the slow, clear, blinding cascade — and I guess we would all like to try that door again, for it seemed like the way, and for a while it *was* the way, the door would open and you would go through winged and exalted (like any rat) and the food would be there, the way the Professor had it arranged, everything OK, and you had chosen the right door, for the world was young. The time they changed that door on me, my nose bled for a hundred hours. I am tired of the jumping and I do not know which way to go.

The idea of "The Door" is about choosing to make choices at all; it is about frustration, and the switching of doors on the rats who are today's choosers.

That story of my own which I cited in an earlier section, called "A Summer's Long Dream," is about a woman frustrated because she is not free to choose. Because she submits to frustration for so long, she is unable to choose to go sailing; she has to settle for a choice made for her, long ago. That crisis consists of a choice made in a state of bondage to the past.

If we take a crisis, a choice, a personality as a criterion of what belongs inside the short story form, then we can perhaps agree that the Book of Jonah in the Bible is, after all, a short story. In it God instructs Jonah to go to Nineveh and reform its people. But Jonah thinks he knows better than God does what he is equipped to do, so he boards a ship going to Tarshish to get away from God. On the voyage a great storm arises in token of God's disapproval of Jonah's evasion, and the sailors throw Jonah overboard, at his own request, to quiet the sea. Instead of drowning, however, he is swallowed by a great fish, as every child can tell. In its belly he has three days and three nights to think things over. Then he chooses that which inevitably he must do. (This seems to me to be at least one meaning of this story.) The fish thereupon vomits Jonah up on dry land, and off he goes to Nineveh and reforms its inmates with such a vengeance that he ends up more wrathful toward them than even the Lord God was, and the story ends on the ironic note that Jonah, who had been shown great mercy, shows so little himself.

On the other hand, that story of Chuang T'zu's about Lieh Tzu pointing to the skull and saying " 'Only you and I know that there is no such thing as life, and no such thing as death' " cannot by these criteria be considered a short story. In fact I myself do not consider it even a story. It is a philosophic aphorism. When readers remark that they like a story in which something *happens,* they are only expressing an innate instinct for the short story in its proper form. What happens need be no more than that crisis of choice. It need only be E. B. White's unidentified I, stepping out of that door — or is it a window?

All works of literary art, in whatever form, aim at totality. They aim to say all that can be said about their particular subject. It is one measure of a good short story if it gives the reader the feeling of having cleaned up what it undertook to deal with, leaving nothing more to tell. After reading such a short story you should be able to feel, as you do feel after reading Chekhov's stories, "I understand now, all about it." A short story could not possibly accomplish this, given some ideas and their meanings. Such ideas may be the sort of statements of pure being which poetry can make, or they may be ideas for novels. It is nothing against the short story form that it can only contain certain kinds of ideas. That is its strength. That is its purpose.

In my youth there was a great deal of talk about the stultifying effects of writing within a form, and a great deal of experimental effort to avoid writing within a form at all. It seems to me that to succeed in this is impossible. *Whatever* way one puts one's writing down becomes its form, whether for good or bad. Form cannot be avoided. Freedom lies more in deciding on what forms are appropriate to what is to be said. We were not advised, in the New Testament, to put new wine in no bottles at all; we were advised to put it in new bottles. A good form is one that is flexible, tough, adaptable, capable of development, ever new. It seems to me that the short story form is all of these things. It is small, economical, and capable of infinite evolution in the technical devices by which it communicates itself to the reader, which devices constitute the third stage of building the short story.

{ *NINE* }

❧

The Short Story: Means of Communication

THE THIRD stage that takes place in the building of a short story is the phase involving communication, and communication involves a number of practical techniques for expressing the idea with which the story began, for showing the idea off to the reader to best advantage, somewhat as a dancer shows off his partner.

As I have said, one of these techniques is beginning the story; another is the balance of forces. I think of this balance as an architectural arrangement of the forces working within a story, whereby humor will be balanced by something heavier that will weight the wit down and keep it from flying entirely out of the story; whereby an implied standard of ethics, for example, can balance the depiction of license. As readers, we ought not to be swamped by such turgid emotions as suffering, anger, passion, if unrelieved by a counterforce in operation. Also under the category of communication I have already placed writing in scenes; the motivation behind action; and that important technique, the making of transitions in time and in subject. Sometimes I have felt that a whole essay might usefully be written about the making of swift and unnoticeable transitions.

Once again let me urge the reader not to let any of these notions persuade him that a short story can possibly be written in three stages — idea, form, and means of communication. They are all involved in the writing of a short story, but they do not occur separately or in sequence. I have put them in this sequence because they seem to follow logically in that order. But to think of them in that order is a convention, and untrue to the reality. They all occur at once, as I have already said, in different degrees. It is impossible to have an idea without some feeling for the form of the idea. It is impossible to entertain a feeling for the form of a story without seeing it in scenes and visualizing the balance of forces that keeps up its tension.

We have been considering the short story hitherto solely from the point of view of the one who writes it; but suppose we start to consider it instead from the point of view of the one who reads it. Why should he want to read it? Why should he submit to going on with it after he has first glanced at it? Reading a short story is purely volunteer work. The fact is that a reader has got to be beguiled, coaxed, and tricked into coming up to the short story, sniffing it, and then settling down to, we hope, enjoying it. As William Maxwell says in *The Writer as Illusionist*, "The reader, skeptical, experienced, with many demands on his time and many ways of enjoying his leisure, is asked to believe in people he knows don't exist, to be present at scenes that never occurred, to be amused or moved or instructed just as he would be in real life, only the life exists in somebody else's imagination." It seems to me that perhaps the most essential trick is to get the reader to start reading the story at all. Young writers, aflame with the importance of what they have to say, often don't realize this.

In the village near where I spend my summers there is a grocery called Ketchopoulos', run by the members of a handsome Greek family, outside which are ranged stalls filled with peaches, bananas, nectarines, grapes, all exquisitely arranged on big grape leaves underneath huge hanging baskets of purple flowers. Everything beckons the prospective purchaser, everything speaks of taste, beauty, and the delights of the palate. The beginning of a short story should be just such a lure and a promise of further delights within. It must be a teaser. It should not offer everything in one fell swoop, of course, but it should offer samples of everything. Just as every sort of fruit is displayed outdoors by the Ketchopouloi, so the beginning of a short story should offer an inventory of special information that will be needed by the reader.

Like the data scientists feed into a computer if it is to give a right answer, a certain percentage of the facts about mood, character, tempo need to be fed into the reader at the beginning if he is ever to find in the short story what the author wants him to find. Young writers often seem to hope their readers will find something miraculous in their short story that they themselves missed, but this seldom actually happens. If, however, the writer knows what he is doing in his story, if he knows what he means, if he knows what he wants his reader to find, it is possible for him to lead his reader, by technical tricks, along the paths which render the most favorable prospect of it.

I would like to give a few examples of good leads to short stories in order to show how wares can be displayed temptingly and artfully. There is, to begin with, the classic lead that gives information on the theme of the story, makes certain promises which the story will fulfill, and gives clues that are needed to find something concealed in it. Such a one is the start of the famous "The Lottery" of Shirley Jackson, a lead which plays completely fair with the reader:

"The morning of June twenty-seventh was clear and sunny, with the fresh warmth of a full-summer day; the flowers were blossoming profusely and the grass was richly green. The people of the village began to gather in the square, between the post-office and the bank, around ten o'clock; in some towns there were so many people that the lottery took two days and had to be started on June twenty-sixth, but in this village, where there were only about three hundred people, the whole lottery took less than two hours, so it could begin at ten o'clock in the morning and still be through in time to allow the villagers to be home for noon dinner."

A great deal of information vital to the story has been transmitted in the course of giving an attractive and intriguing come-on. The reader knows all he needs to know to proceed, at the same time that his curiosity has been whetted as to what kind of lottery this can possibly be. A similarly informative beginning is that of Chekhov's "An Upheaval":

"Mashenka Pavletsky, a young girl who had only just finished her studies at a boarding-school, returning from a walk to the house of the Kushkins, with whom she was living as a governess, found the household in a terrible turmoil. Mihailo, the porter who opened the door to her, was excited and red as a crab. Loud voices were heard from upstairs. 'Madame Kushkin is in a fit, most likely, or else she has quarrelled with her husband,' thought Mashenka."

The reader has been informed of what he needs to know about Mashenka, her age, history, position in life, and the way her mind works, at the same time that he has been plunged into an upheaval from which it is most doubtful that he can, any longer, extricate himself. Such another beginning is that of Sylvia Townsend Warner's "The Phoenix."

"Lord Strawberry, a nobleman, collected birds. He had the finest aviary in Europe, so large that eagles did not find it uncomfortable, so well laid out that both humming-birds and snow-buntings had a climate that suited them perfectly. But for many years the finest set of apartments remained empty, with just a label saying, 'Phoenix. Habitat: Arabia.'"

A different sort of beguilement is offered by the beginning which might be called the character-situation lead, like the start of Eudora Welty's "Death of a Travelling Salesman":

"R. J. Bowman, who for fourteen years had travelled for a shoe company through Mississippi, drove his Ford along a rutted dirt path. It was a long day! The time did not seem to clear the noon hurdle and settle into soft afternoon. The sun, keeping its strength here even in winter, stayed at the top of the sky, and every time Bowman stuck his head out of the car to stare up the road, it seemed to reach a long arm down and push against the top of his head, right through his hat — like the joke of an old drummer, long on the road. It made him feel all the more angry and helpless. He was feverish, and he was not quite sure of the way."

How can we possibly leave poor Mr. Bowman now? Or take

quite a different kind of beginning, that of John O'Hara's "Graven Image":

"The car turned in at the brief, crescent-shaped drive and waited until the two cabs ahead had pulled away. The car pulled up, the doorman opened the rear door, a little man got out. The little man nodded pleasantly enough to the doorman and said 'Wait' to the chauffeur. 'Will the Under Secretary be here long?' asked the doorman.

" 'Why?' said the little man.

" 'Because if you were going to be here, sir, only a short while, I'd let your man leave the car here, at the head of the rank.'

" 'Leave it there *anyway*,' said the Under Secretary."

What, we want to know, we have to know, is *he* up to?

The point I am trying to establish here, by giving these examples of successful beginnings, is related to the Toynbeean principle of withdrawal and return set forth in a later section. Of the three stages I have described in the building of the short story, the first constitutes a withdrawal into the self for contemplation of the idea and what it may mean; the second, a gradual feeling the way into what the proper form to contain the idea, together with its meaning, may be; but the third, that of technical means of communication, represents the phase of return, in that it considers those outside to be communicated with; it plots ways of beguiling the outsider to listen to the communication; it takes into account the likes and dislikes and probable reactions of the outsider — as that a start to a perfectly good story may prove boring if care is not taken to make it interesting.

This point is applicable to the matter of balance of forces as well, if one is to make one's private idea understood by other people. I feel strongly that a short story, successfully communicated, must be architecturally planned. It can, for example, be ruined by an overemphasis on plot that acts like a top-heavy cornice to detract from the design. If it has a wing to one side — say a comic character — it must have a wing to the other. This goes not only for weight of attention given to one character, group of characters, or a situation in a short story, but it also goes for the balance which is a more delicate thing — the balance of values. Much may be learned by noticing the wonderful, urbane, misleadingly tea-table discourse in both the novels and the short stories of E. M. Forster, which is balanced by the most extraordinarily violent happenings — thriller happenings. Such a balance acts like an armature in sculpture. Upon it the short story supports its weight, and I believe that unless the balance is there, the short story will fall flat on its face.

Most outstanding short stories, when considered from this point of view, will be found to be as carefully balanced as weight-scales. Since we are speaking of matters principally technical, let us consider that master technician, Rudyard Kipling. The student of writing should never allow prejudices about imperialism to stand in the way of his picking Kipling's brains. The least of his tales communicates what it was he was trying to communicate.

One of Kipling's great specialties was the balance of forces. Take a story called "Bimi," which is not even one of the famous stories. In it, a German named Hans Breitman tells the "I" of the story about his friend Bertran in Malaya, who had owned and tamed an orangutan. Breitman tells this story on a ship crossing the Indian Ocean, and he is reminded of it by the presence on board of another orangutan, which is being shipped to a circus. Throughout Kipling's narrative, this creature, "troubled by some dream of the forests of his freedom, yelled like a soul in purgatory, and wrenched madly at the bars of his cage." Breitman's tale concerns the absolute trust that Bertran reposed in his pet, and how when he got married to a very pretty girl, his confidence was complete that the ape would love the bride as much as he loved his master. Hans Breitman warned Bertran, he says, that the creature was jealous and dangerous; but Bertran replied, "He will obey and love my wife, and if she speaks he will get out her slippers." He is so sure that he leaves the girl alone with the orangutan. When he returns, with Breitman, it is to find, inside the room into which the girl had tried to lock herself away, "nothing in the room that could be called a woman. There was stuff on the floor, and that was all." Breitman, telling of this confrontation, compares what was left to paper in a wastebasket, or cards at whist when scattered over the table. In retaliation, the husband catches the ape and kills him with his own hands, even though the ratio of strength in the orangutan is more than seven to man's one.

This story (which is not without its subtlety; what was this German bridegroom doing, trusting his monster as above his bride? And why must he revenge himself on a savage creature for being natural?) would be perhaps too fantastically gory in the hands of a less skillful writer, but Kipling's German tells the whole tale with a thick accent. Even when things get most grisly, this accent cuts the grease of the gruesomeness — "When I come back, der ape he was dead, and Bertran he was dying abofe him; but still he laughed, a liddle and low, and he was quite content. Bertran, he haf killed Bimi mit sooch things as Gott giff him" (and proved his own primitive strength to be equal to his monster's). This comedy accent keeps the ghastly doings, possibly allegorical of the German divided psyche, down on the level of reality. Lest the accent descend to *low* comedy, Kipling endows Breitman with a strange, compelling power over the actual ape in the present of the story, howling in his cage on deck: "From Hans's mouth issued an imitation of a snake's hiss, so perfect I almost sprang to my feet. The murderous sound ran along the deck and the wrenching at the bars ceased. The orang-outan was quaking in an ecstasy of pure terror." We cannot wholly laugh at a man who has the power to quell orangutans; and it springs to our mind to wonder if he has told the whole story of his relation to Bertran, his bride and that other ape. Horror against comedy relief, comedy relief against respect for a sinister authority — this tale is an example of the artful balancing of forces.

The opposite — a lack of balance — is, I think, to be found in most unsuccessful short stories. This may be the result of one-sidedness of conception. The simplest way to explain what I mean is to say that one should not write about any force in terms of that force. Thus, it is fatal to write of anger angrily, or of sorrow mournfully. This is the opposite of balance; this is one-sidedness. Although I admire the novels of Ellen Glasgow, when I read her posthumous autobiography, *The Woman Within,* I was repelled by her continual insistence, in agonized tones, on how much she had suffered, using the word "suffer" to insist on it with. I am sorry that Ellen Glasgow, the woman, had to suffer as she did; but as a reader I react against her manner of telling about it.

It is a truism that the humorist is basically a man of sorrows — Pagliacci and Thurber are prototypes. At the heart of this insight lies the recognition of the necessary balance between humor and tragedy, tears and laughter. Children instantly respond to solemnity by acting silly; even grown up, I find that if anyone talks in sufficiently elegant tones to me my instinct is to assume a Brooklyn accent in reply. One of the best ways to write about horror is to be callous about it, as we have just seen Kipling do; the horror seeps through all the more horribly for not being dwelt upon. It is even effective to be funny about illness. In my novel *Heaven and Hardpan Farm*, a sanitariumfull of neurotic ladies feel very ill indeed; but some things are so painful, and so depressing, that it is as though there were nothing left to do *but* to laugh. In writing the book, I laughed — but with a great deal of affection — at the loveless ladies of Hardpan Farm. What is not effective is to be sentimental about sentiment, moral about morality, pained by the painful.

That old nonesuch W. Somerset Maugham, who, whether one admires his work or not, can give pointers on technique to his betters any day, furnishes many an example of the expert balancing of forces. Let us examine his short story "A String of Beads."

This slight tale has a melodramatic plot. A governess in England is by accident given by a jeweler, in exchange for her cheap imitation pearls she had left for stringing, a necklace worth fifty thousand pounds. When the jeweler discovers his mistake he offers her a reward for the return of the real pearls. The governess accepts the reward and gives up the fortune that has been within her hands and around her throat. She quits her post and goes to the Continent for a holiday, to spend the reward and live like a duchess for four weeks. While on her vacation she meets a rich South American whose mistress she becomes. In the end she becomes a high-class courtesan in Paris.

This is all perhaps too lurid to seem credible if it were told luridly, or even seriously. But Maugham has put his story into the mouth of an upper-class, conventional, nitwit narrator, a friend of the governess's fashionable mistress. This lady views the whole episode in such class-conscious terms as to balance the melodrama every step of the way and lend real point to the tale. At the very first, the narrator suspects the governess of having stolen the real pearls. When the governess accepts the reward and returns the necklace, the narrator (herself bejeweled) comments that it is, after all, the very least she could do. When the governess departs for the Continent to spend the reward, the narrator considers this an unsuitable and pretentious plan for a person of that class, who should be saving her money. When the governess winds up in a life of sin, the narrator concludes that this must have been the sort of woman she was all along.

The interesting thing is that by balancing the governess with the callous and unsympathetic society narrator, Maugham can tell us a very complete story — an overtly sensational tale with an inner meaning which has to do with a governess's life being so thankless that a life of sin may well seem preferable. Maugham makes us see the pathos and the irony of the governess's life as we should never have done if he had told us she was touching, if he had informed us that her story was pathetic or ironic. He never told us, but he has shown us the absurdity, in human terms, of class distinctions.

A beginning writer who plans to put into his story anything very positive or definite or strong should ask himself what it will be balanced by. It appears to be human nature to look for, to require, a balance; readers do this in every story they read, whether they know what it is they require or not. I have already spoken of how young writers may even find it helps sometimes to make a drawing of the architectural shape of the story, to see what a proper balance would look like. Such a drawing might look like a circle with two horns at the top, or a house with twin chimneys, or three mountains with valleys between.

In "A String of Beads," the characters are first shown to the reader at a dinner party where the governess, who has been invited downstairs to fill in, is wearing, all unaware, the real pearls. This is a beginning which plunges us at once into a scene gay, urbane, and sophisticated. It is like Maugham to have given us something to visualize which we will enjoy visualizing. While it is not necessary that a short story be laid in scenes as alluring as Maugham's dinner party or exotic as Kipling's Indian Ocean, it *is* essential that it be presented so that it can be seen, and clearly. Hearing the story is not enough.

Last spring I spoke before a class in "creative writing" whose members later read aloud some of their recent efforts. The first story was about a farmer and his wife; how their son married a girl that the wife didn't like, but how they all came to shake down together passably enough in the end. There is nothing the matter with that as a short story, if you could be made to see it. All that is needed is for its author to be sufficiently excited about what he sees in his mind's eye to go to the trouble of finding ways to make other people see what he sees. The story began something like this:

"John Jameson lived on a cow farm at the end of the village of Weatherby. His wife, Anna, was an efficient woman about the house, about fifty years old. They had one son, Jed, who was courting a girl by the name of Liza Jenkins, who was a pretty girl who loved to skate." There is nothing the matter with that as a beginning, either; I took to the girl who loved to skate at once. But the trouble was that the story continued, throughout, in the same narrative vein. It never settled down so that you could look at the people against some definite setting. It told you everything that happened to these four people, but it showed you almost nothing. Its author had not visualized her story.

When I was invited to comment on the story I suggested that it might be more effective if written in scenes. This seemed to strike the author as a completely new idea. Since I find it impossible to believe that the instructor of the writing class had never spoken about the importance of this time-honored technical device, I can only conclude that some beginning writers have a real resistance to writing in scenes.

The fact is, however, that it is hard to listen for very long, whether you are being read to or are reading to yourself. It is much easier and more vivid to see. The author who can make us see his story as it happened, as an event, with only a minimum of informative connecting transitions, is the author into whose arms we fall with cries of joy and relief after we have been reading stories, of whatever integrity, written with no gift of seeing. To be able to conceive a story in terms of seeing instead of telling is actually a function of the author's feeling rather than of his technique, which shows how inextricably intertwined the elements of a short story are. An idea for a story, a design for a shape into which it may be put, and the technical means of communicating the story are, in effect, like the bare skeleton of an ego, with no love. Nothing can be done until feeling has come to fill out the flesh and blood of a story. But even if a short story is written for the most mechanical of reasons, as plot, without love, it must still present itself through scenes that the reader can in fancy move into or the chances are that it will not present itself at all.

When one takes a swift glance back over impressive short stories, it is not by their prose that one remembers them, nor even entirely by their characterizations. One remembers first of all the scenes they presented — the hotel dining room in which Carson McCullers' jockey chewed up the mouthful of French-fried potatoes and spat it out on the red carpet; the cottage fireside with the two boys beside it getting tight on whisky and talking, in Hemingway's "The Three Day Blow"; the tubercular American mother holding out her arms alone and dancing around her son's bedroom, in "My Mother Dancing" by G. T. Huntington; the bathroom with the son shaving in it and the mother sitting talking to him in Salinger's "Zooey."

Why did Carson McCullers' jockey spit the food out on the floor? Why does the hero of Irwin Shaw's "Main Currents of American Thought" put up with so much from his family? Why is Faulkner's Nancy so afraid to go home to her cabin alone, in "That Evening Sun"? If the writer will establish a strong enough motive for action in his short story, he has established a life-line over which almost anything can be carried. If he fails to establish a strong and acceptable motive, he can save his best writing and his keenest observations; they will not help. In discussing the elements of a short story, it is in one sense unnecessary to discuss action at all. If strong enough motives are provided, rooted in the hearts and nerves of the characters, action will automatically follow. It is just as in real life, given enough fear or anger or desire a man cannot fail to take the inevitable step and act on them. Action follows on motive. One may, indeed, when analyzing behavior, whether fictional or real, seek motive *behind* action; but when we are working in the other direction (the direction concerned with the successful communication of an idea and its meaning within a form in the mind of a writer, over and across into the mind of a reader), we may take it as an axiom that motive, satisfactorily established, leads to action.

Faulkner said once at the University of Virginia that he never plots out the actions of his characters but rather, as he put it, runs "along behind them writing down what they do and say." This giving autonomy to fictional characters, which I think Faulkner meant seriously and hardly figuratively at all, is of course a rejection of responsibility for possessing an unconscious that amounts almost to animism. But it is certainly true that Faulkner's characters have an energy seldom equaled in literature. What they do or don't do flows spontaneously out of the passions which so powerfully motivate them. The terror, agony, and despair with which Nancy appeals to her white family in "That Evening Sun" well up out of the fatal devotion she bears for Jesus, her husband. She cannot possibly run away, move, or do anything but just wait for him to cut her throat with a razor whenever he finally comes out of the surrounding darkness. In "A Rose for Emily," Miss Emily was driven to the crime which she committed so long ago, and which we discover at the story's end, by a pride which is her besetting motive. It was inconceivable to her, impossible, that she would allow herself to be jilted.

The motives of love for his friend maimed in a race-track accident, and outrage at the indifference displayed by trainer and owner, are what drive Mrs. McCullers' jockey to eat, to drink, to do all a jockey should not do, before his culminating outburst when he rejects, by spitting out, all that the rest of the world does. Andrew, in "Main Currents of American Thought," puts up with the burdens his family heap upon him out of the touching conscious motive of wanting to be a decent person and the at least understandable and less conscious one of not wanting to start trouble. The acts that spring out of such motives can be, often are, far from admirable. They may be nothing the reader would care to think himself capable of. But the motives that inspired the acts — those we must be able to identify with. Love, pride, loyalty, fear — these are all universal wellsprings of human action. When acts resulting from them turn out shocking, melodramatic, pathetic, horrible, contemptible even, we might shrink from performing similar acts in our lives, but we can accept them in the short story. We would not be able to accept them unless we could accept the premise of their motives.

Lately I was asked to read a short story by a woman writer about her childhood in Italy, and of how, when she went away from her village to visit her priest uncle in another village, one morning it suddenly came over her how beautiful is the country in Tuscany. The feeling conveyed by the story was delicate, even exquisite. But one could not refrain from asking, Why does the central character receive her illumination while visiting this uncle? Is it because she felt confined at home? Is it because she is in particular sympathy with her uncle? We are never shown so, nor allowed to gather as much. It is true that in real life this is how it might happen — fortuitously (although in real life there is always a cause too, hidden or not). But this is not life; this is fiction. In fiction there has to be a *reason* for events, and this reason is called motive. If we saw that the girl had felt tied down at home, and in the freedom of escaping to her uncle's, perhaps after an evening of talk with him, had then received her flash of perception, that would supply a motive; even though the motive were supplied unnoticeably, by inference—as indeed it ought to be. But it was not even implied. The word *motive* comes from the Latin *movere*, to move; and it is indeed motive alone which moves a story along, keeps it coming, through the various ups and downs which befall its characters.

If it is motive which keeps the story coming, it is the technique of making transitions which gets it up the ups and down the downs. Ideally, you should never know when you are reading a transition. It should fool you. You should be under the impression that you have been reading straight along without a break, but that somehow you have been conveyed, as by what science fiction calls teleportation, from Italy to the United States, or from midnight to noon a year later. How this was accomplished you should not be able to say. It ought to be pure trickery; magic.

At the bottom of making a transition in the short story lies the bridge sentence or bridge paragraph. This is a sentence or paragraph which leads the reader from one time to another, one place to another, or one subject to another in such a way that he is unaware of being budged. Here is an example of bridge sentences from a story of my own called "The King of Fancy's Daughter": "Dusk was now trembling on the verges of the hills, and Isabel found herself assessing it in terms of the dusk of last night's events. It was not as dim now as then — not nearly." We have been moved from tonight back to last night, which is essential to the story, by our identification with Isabel, who does the contrasting of the two evenings. We are not required to make the move; she does it for us.

"Isabel shut the door softly and went to her room. It had been her parents', when she was a little girl, before they had begun having separate bedrooms." We have been teleported in space not only over the distance between the front door and the bedroom, but between today and twenty years ago. Again Isabel did the work.

"Life was a dream, I thought; no, a nightmare. I was still in this state, half-sulking and half-exalted, when Mr. Hubert Timberlake came to the town." We have been moved into the events that will follow upon Mr. Timberlake's arrival, from those which went before it, entirely by way of a small boy's moods. "We waited for Mr. Timberlake to come downstairs. I put on white flannels and soon I was walking down to the river with Mr. Timberlake." By such devious transitions as these, V. S. Pritchett makes it possible for himself to bring this story, "The Saint," to a conclusion where he has earned the right to treat us to a great, roaring switch — not a proper transition at all but a good old-fashioned "Sixteen years have passed since I dropped Mr. Timberlake in the river."

Another use of the transition is telescoping. Much can get accomplished and stuck away out of sight within the confines of a sentence or two, leaving us free to get on with the story.

"Driving the children before her up the stairs, Isabel reflected that the very qualities that are most enchanting in children are most irritating in the old. When Bella and Willy were tucked away into the twin beds of her own childhood, like rosy apples into dumplings, she switched out the old hanging light." About three-quarters of an hour's work and a train of thought have been compressed into two sentences.

Then there is the sentence that must effect a transition in subject: "Behind the drifting mists of memory, her own present still hammered like horses and thundered like ocean." We have been plucked up out of the past and stuck down into the present. Faulkner's "That Evening Sun" begins with a three-paragraph description of the Negro washerwomen of Jefferson, including one named Nancy, carrying bundles of clothes on their heads; how they did it and how they looked doing it. The fourth paragraph begins with this sentence: "Sometimes the husbands of the washing women would fetch and deliver the clothes, but Jesus never did that for Nancy, even before Father told him to stay away from our house; even when Dilsey was sick and Nancy would come to cook for us." The amount of information in that one sentence is amazing. Besides having been moved out of a generalized consideration of Jefferson into the events of the story, we have been given actually everything the story is going to be about, including some characterization of Jesus.

The sentences I have used as examples sound simple. If they did not sound simple they would not be good transition sentences. They are all of them art in the sense of being artful. They use tricks. All techniques are tricks. Like a backhand at tennis, or making crisp pastry, or applying nail-polish dexterously, techniques are something that can be learned. Ideally they should also, after being learned, be put out of mind, just as one does not think, in walking, that walking is just repeatedly losing one's balance and catching it again. Techniques should turn into being ease. My father used to say, about painting, "Technique is the ease that comes to the master."

Above all, techniques should not be thought of as separate entities, ends in themselves. They are only methods or means to an end, the end being the perfected backhand, the light-as-air pastry, or, in this case, the fulfilled short story. As I have said again and again in the course of these sections, the short story must be thought of as a whole, never, heretically, as balanced forces or powerful motives or skillful transitions. The short story, with all its parts, might be thought of as if it were Yeats's chestnut tree — "great-rooted blossomer,/Are you the leaf, the blossom, or the bole?"

❦

TEN

A Note on Feeling

I SEE that in a foregoing section I laid myself open to mis-interpretation by saying, "An idea for a story, a design for a shape into which it may be put, and the technical means of communicating the idea are . . . like the bare bones of an ego, with no love. Nothing can be done until feeling has come to fill out the flesh and blood of a story." These sentences could suggest the image of a dam site, carefully logged over and prepared, into which dammed-up water is all at once released with a sound like thunder. No image could less convey the role feeling plays in the creation of fiction. To get right down to it, feeling must be there even before the idea takes shape. In the beginning of fiction was, not the word, but the feeling.

The novelist John Knowles, lecturing on writing at the University of Virginia, spoke of how his novel *A Separate Peace* first came to him in the form of feeling for a grove of trees in New Hampshire. In the question period that followed, a student asked him how he had gone about analyzing his feel-ing for the trees so as to find the story. The speaker replied that he didn't analyze his feeling at all; he made a novel out of it. One of the things about the art of writing fiction that appears most difficult to put across is concerned with this point: that creative writing, unlike criticism, is not analytic in its methods, but synthetic. Creative writing does not take feelings apart, it puts them together. This seems to me a simple enough concept, yet again and again in speaking of it one is met by kindly, intelligent, but uncomprehending faces.

In the beginning *has* to have been the feeling. The writer, actually, is one who goes around in a state which has been described as skinlessness. This is the "state of open susceptibility" which Elizabeth Bowen speaks of. It is a state of being hardly to be dignified by the name of love; it is, even, distantly akin to far less reputable states. Supersensitivity, touchiness, liability to take everything personally are some forms subjectivity takes in people unequipped to do something with it, people who fluctuate between the sterile alternatives of inferior and superior; who are not artists, to use the broader term. The writer is, precisely, one who does know what to do with his subjectivity. In this state, which can be as well of exaltation as of gloom, objects along his day's path — sights, sounds, smells, a taste, touch — impinge upon his fragile sentience and reach painful or thrilling fingers into the depth of his being.

The earliest recollection I have of needing to write anything is of when I was about eight, sitting on the back steps of our house after a rain, staring out at the swamp that was purple with loosestrife and joe-pye weed. A cat came skulking out of the long wet grass and wove its way past the steps, rubbing its sides against the rough boards. I couldn't bear it. After a while I went back into the house, and in my journal — my "Diary. Private. Keep Out!" which had hitherto been filled only with accounts of meetings of the Four Queens Club and of swimming at Lake Pearl — I began, "As I was sitting on the back steps today, a cat came skulking out of the long wet grass. . . ."

Feeling is so essential in the writing of fiction as to be like charity in First Corinthians: if the writer hasn't got it, he is nothing. The reason for this may be that feeling for fiction — or indeed for anything else — is the same as belief in it. If the writer doesn't believe in his own fictions he is certainly not going to persuade the reader to believe in all that imitation grass, bogus activity, and imaginary conversation. If he does have feeling for his fictions, if he masters the tricks of conveying his feeling without too much interfering with it, a light will go up on the scene he has set, the blindfold will be snatched from his readers' eyes, and, purring with delight, they will set themselves to the willing suspension of disbelief.

I have never felt that the literal taking of notes by a writer went very far in creating characters that came alive. A writer in New Hampshire was telling me how he makes careful notes of every interesting event or person or scene that comes his way and then transfers the scribbled notes by typing them out on file cards. Next he inserts the cards into their proper places in a file-case and, he said, he has five of these file-cases already filled with notes on every aspect of life. He has really pinned experience down. But I must confess I have more confidence in Mr. Faulkner's system of running along after characters who originated in his imagination and writing down what *they* say. It may not be so neat, but it is a lot more like being a writer. The writer who files his notes has everything put away safely where he can find it again, but Mr. Faulkner has feeling for his characters — and, need I add, it profiteth him.

Feeling, not emotion. Similar to the people who don't believe in fiction, who can't seem to grasp that a writer can "make it all up," are the people who insist on using the word "feeling" interchangeably with the word "emotion," as if they were the same quality. They are certainly allied; but feeling, as I am speaking of it here, is neither hate, fear, anger, nor desire; it is a method of perceiving. It is concerned with secrets, with hiding-places, with inventions, with phantasy; with imaginary people and imaginary conversations. I remember once finding myself alone at dinner in a New York club, tired after a long day, looking about the roomful of men and women, for the most part elderly, and being slowly filled with an enormous delight, not in them as real people, but in them as characters. It could hardly have been called love — I knew nobody present — it was more an ecstasy of examining those idiosyncratic old faces, mentally caressing their withered arms, admiring their necklaces and their tortoise-shell crosses on chains, their black satin dresses, their too-soft white hair, their pink scalps, their old fingers loaded with diamond rings, the glittering crystal of their pince-nez; a side-comb about to tumble here, a spot of gravy upon a starched shirt-front there; an ambassadorial mustache, a hairdo of looped-up gray scallops above an intellectual brow, a mink cape thrown back over a chair, a gray woolen dress wholly unsuitable for dining; a copy of Plato laid by the plate of one solitary diner, a scarlet brocade purse beside the plate of another; an important frown, an experienced laugh; frowsty old eyebrows lifted knowingly, an air of firm, forthright address delivered with no nonsense, tinklingly sweet tones, a voice overheard saying, "My dear . . . ," another voice that whined, " 'Her-bert,' I told him, 'that just won't do!' " They were so marvelous. I was full of joy. This may have been partly feeling for life, but it was mostly feeling for fiction.

Feeling's function is to inform its possessor of what things mean to him. (It is in this sense that I called meaning, in another section, the further side of idea.) Unlike emotion, which is not a conscious function at all, it gropes, touches, caresses, explores; although it is so wholly absorbed in the meanings of things, it is thing-centered, not, like emotion, self-centered. Emotion inundates, like that thunderous dam-water; but it is feeling's whole nature to discriminate, to select. Feeling plays with the scene — and perhaps this is the safest definition of all for the kind of feeling a writer needs: a feeling for play with the materials of experience.

At that lecture of John Knowles's to which I have already referred, he was asked why writers view critics as their enemies. (One arch questioner put it, "Mr. Knowles, you will concede, I presume, that the well-disposed critic can be the writer's friend?") The speaker replied that the trouble is, critics are so much more intelligent than writers, writers can't really understand them. There was some dissatisfied shifting about in seats at this. Yet it is true that fiction simply cannot proceed from the intellect — a fact known to the wisest old editors, who, in making suggestions for change, try to soothe their authors' feelings rather than to challenge their minds. For some time it has been fashionable to salaam before intellect and all its doings, and most people today either lead with the intellect or play like they are doing so. There are some things the intellect cannot do, however, and one of them is, unaided, to write a good story. A friend of mine, one of the dozen best short story writers in the country, told me she learned how to write short stories from being in love, at different times, with two men who wrote short stories. Not that they told her much. It just came off on her.

The novelist Rosamond Lehmann writes, "I am surpised when writers have perfectly clear ideas for what they are going to write, and I find it dismaying, for more reasons than one, to have the projected contents related to me, at length and in rational sequence. I would be more encouraged by such an answer — given in rather a hostile and depressed way — as: It is about some people. And if the author could bear to pursue the subject, and mention any of the images and symbols haunting his mind — if he spoke for instance of a fin turning in a waste of waters, of the echo in the caves, of an empty house shuttered under dust sheets, of an April fall of snow, of music from the fair at night, of the burnt-out shell of a country house, of that woman seen for a moment from a bus-top, brushing her hair before the glass — I should feel that something was afoot." Something would indeed be afoot, for all this is the stuff of feeling, which clothes itself, at least in fiction, with symbols and snatches of vision.

Often, moreover, the writer himself — hostile, even frightened, adrift among today's sea of critical minds — tends to identify with the critical approach, which is not at all the same thing as developing the ability to think. So the writer becomes not a critic but an apostate artist. The writer is not incapable of thought, any more than the critic is incapable of feeling; some critics evidence very deep feeling indeed. But the critic's feeling is for finished works of art, not for the imaginary stuff of art (else, perhaps, they would be not critics but writers). For a natural writer to strain to emulate the critic's approach is an expense of spirit in a waste of shame; it is a selling of his birthright. The writer normally lives on feelings, intuitions, and symbols, a state of mind difficult to make believable in real life to even the kindliest critical intelligence. His art consists of the overcoming of this barrier by a supreme act of transference. If he fails in his task, he may become one of those artists who claim to despise the intellect and all its works. But this is no victory, for only false pride despises its opposite.

It is as though once upon a time there was a forest, which was approached at opposite sides by two brothers. The older brother came up to the forest, examined its appearance meticulously from various angles, peered into it, drew out a notebook, and set down some notes in which he commented on the forest's vast extent, overgrown condition, and likelihood of containing snakes. He then walked away, having understood the forest. The younger brother approached the forest and, his fancy at once captured by the sight of a lichen growing on the silver-gilt bark of a birch tree just inside, plunged into the woods and in no time at all was lost. Treading on treacherous and swampy ground, hemmed in on every side by bristling primeval tree-trunks, threatened by poisonous serpents that hung from the branches of the trees, too far inside to call for help, it took every particle of ingenuity he possessed to figure out the way to get back again. At last, however, he did emerge, and with quite a story to tell. It is so with the writer, faced by experience.

This parable is of course misleading, because the older

brother, the critic, is viewing the experience of real facts, real finished forests and books, when he takes his notes. For his writing brother, moreover, the perils of the forest exist largely in his own imagination. The tree-trunks were, possibly, papier-mâché; the snakes, rubber hose; the critic brother would never have allowed himself to become so panicky. Yet that is the way the writer is. He needs every bit of technical wisdom — tricks of telling, organization of method — he can summon if he is to rescue himself from his experience, if he is to persuade any-body else of what happened to him. His thinking self is thus employed in the service of his feeling self, and not, as with his critic brother, in soberly viewing outer reality — whether real life or real books — and coming to conclusions about it.

Form and technique are the salvation of those who, like the writer, feel threatened with inundation by the forces released by experience. They constitute the artist's kind of thinking. A similar salvation used to be the technique of draftmanship in the painter's art, or the technique of manners in society — which used, in fact, to be called "good form." For some, there are the forms of a lifetime's habits, or the ritual forms of the church. The writer, unable to find satisfaction in any order he can discover in or impose upon life, creates his own forms, something to put his experience in. The writer needs form because he cannot contain himself.

"At the end of his writing day," William Maxwell says in his essay on the tricks of writing fiction, "the writer, looking green with fatigue — also from not having shaved — emerges from his narrative dream at last, with something in his hand he wants somebody to listen to. His wife will have to stop what she is doing and think of a card, any card; or be sawed in half again and again until the act is letter-perfect. And when the writer is in bed with the light out, he tosses. Far from dropping off to sleep he thinks of something, and the light beside his bed goes on, long enough for him to write down five words that may or may not mean a great deal to him in the morning. The light may go on and off several times before his steady breathing indicates that he is asleep. And while he is asleep he may dream — he may dream that he had a dream, in which the whole meaning of what he is trying to say is brilliantly revealed to him. Just so the dog asleep on the hearth-rug dreams; you can see, by the faint jerking movement of his four legs, that he is after a rabbit. The writer's rabbit is the truth — about life, about human character, about himself and there-fore by extension, it is to be hoped, about other people. He is convinced that all this is knowable, can be described, can be recorded, by a person sufficiently dedicated to describing and recording; can be caught in a net of narration."

Yet, all rabbits aside, is it really the truth the writer is after, in his imagining, in his play? The writer, as easily in-timidated as he is exalted by words, finds, if he thinks about it, that the word "truth" becomes monolithic, formidable. Is that really what he was trying to convey about his dear trove of sea-shells, his handful of wildflowers from the wood, his private joke? Truth? Possibly if he were Tolstoi. . . . But let me quote one more excerpt, this time from Hemingway's short story "The Three Day Blow." The two adolescent boys, drinking whisky before the fire, have become quite tight. They have been talking about literature.

"Gentlemen," Bill said, "I give you Chesterton and Walpole."

"Exactly, gentlemen," Nick said.

They drank. Bill filled up the glasses again.

"You were very wise, Wemedge," Bill said.

"What do you mean?" asked Nick.

"To bust off that Marge business," Bill said.

"I guess so," said Nick.

"It was the only thing to do. If you hadn't, by now you'd be back working, trying to get enough money to get married."

Nick said nothing.

"Once a man's married he's absolutely bitched," Bill went on. "He hasn't got anything more. Nothing. Not a damn thing. He's done for. You've seen the guys that get married."

Nick said nothing.

"You can tell them," Bill said. "They get this sort of fat, married look. They're done for."

"Sure," said Nick.

"You came out of it damned well," Bill said. "Now she can marry somebody of her own sort and settle down and be happy. You can't mix oil and water, and you can't mix that sort of thing, any more than if I'd marry Ida that works for the Strattons. She'd probably like it, too."

Nick said nothing. The liquor had all died out of him and left him alone. Bill wasn't there. He wasn't sitting in front of the fire, or going fishing tomorrow with Bill and his dad, or anything. He wasn't drunk. It was all gone. All he knew was that he had once had Marjorie and that he had lost her.

That is pure feeling, all right, laid bare before our eyes. It is feeling being revealed by the ultimate in prestidigitation — the art of communicating meaning in terms utterly artless. Hemingway thought that particular trick up for himself; all the best tricks are the ones writers have invented for themselves out of their need. Although it is certainly truth that Hemingway is communicating in this passage, it is neither monolithic nor formidable. It is just something worth trying to say. It is just true.

❦

ELEVEN

The Writing of Autobiographical Fiction

IN AN earlier section when I was talking about characterization in the novel, I said that there are two sources for
ideas for characters — outside observation and the various aspects of oneself. Oneself is not to be sneezed at as a source of
ideas for characters. Far from being just one person — just old
I, that familiar soul so fond of putting her foot in her mouth
— I am made up, as all human beings are, of dozens of fragments glued together by the grace of God into a person. Any
one of these fragments is capable of producing a fully integrated character in fiction.

A friend of mine once wrote a novel which she told me was
peopled by the three primary aspects of herself. Yet the critics
said of the novel that it presented strongly contrasted types
of modern woman who were in conflict with each other's
philosophies. At the same time that my friend told me she had
based all these contrasting characters on aspects of herself, she
had added, "Sometimes I feel as if I had lived three lifetimes."

I think we all sometimes feel that way — one's childhood is so remote; one's youth so far in the past; one's mistakes so irremediable; one's several parts so irreconcilable.

I want to mention now a whole fresh category of fiction. There is, besides the fiction which is based on bits of oneself, each bit grown, as it were, into a whole character, an additional type of fiction: the fiction of so-called autobiography. I say so-called, because I have done a good deal of this kind of fiction in the form of short stories based on my own childhood, and I am thus in a position to report that the autobiography in them was strongly tempered by imagination. In fact, the imagination in them was stronger than the actual memories. I can't believe, either, that the real Columbus, Ohio, of Thurber's boyhood was much like the one we read about.

It is true that what impels writers to write this type of story is a kind of nostalgia. Yet when I come to write such a story, I always find that what is causing me the nostalgia is less any real event or condition of my childhood than the mood of the present. I am able in the end to capture the atmosphere of the past, if I do capture it, less by remembering than by inventing; less by calling up than by making up. It is as if to capture that atmosphere I have to create it, because in fact it never was on land or sea, least of all in my own childhood. Of course, physical facts from my own past *are* in the stories. I want to say a little, as a sequel to my section about characterization, about things to do and things to avoid when utilizing that second source of character material, oneself, and I thought I would use as an example the autobiographical short story.

A woman came up to me the other day at a cocktail party in Virginia and said, "I don't see why you have all those pieces about your childhood published in the *New Yorker*, when *I* don't! I had a *much* more interesting childhood than you seem to have had. I could ride bareback and do a jackknife dive before I was eight, and my greatuncle was one of Lee's scouts." "Well," I said, "I'm sure you're right. Why don't you write about it all?" She looked appalled. "Oh," she said. "How do I know anybody would be interested?"

So I asked a reading friend what it is that she hopes for when she reads a work of autobiography — what it is she wants to find in it. She replied flatly that she hoped most anxiously of all not to be bored, and added that she was just plain not interested in reading about anyone's life unless he happened to be Roosevelt or Winston Churchill. She said that when she did pick up a work of autobiographical writing she hoped to heaven she wasn't going to have to read in detail of the life of somebody who meant nothing to her, who had no associations for her.

Now it is my view, too, that, unless the author is Roosevelt or Winston Churchill, nobody will be much interested in hearing about his life. Therefore the writer has to make him interested. An Anglo-Irish literary agent once made a remark about an early autobiographical story of mine, years ago, that gave me a real shock. He said, "Nobody is interested in Miss Hale's opinions." Autobiographical writing, if it is to be interesting, simply must not give the impression of being filled with its author's opinions. What, then, is it to be filled with? What is the point of writing autobiographically? What are the purposes?

There is, of course, and not to be laughed off, the author's own need to write about himself. There is such a thing as needing to talk about oneself, out loud, in public. Something is crying out to be said, and somehow it cannot be said in conversation, or in letters. Of this particular need, I may say that the nature of the need usually is not known until the need has been satisfied. That is, once the author has talked out loud and in public about his life, he may then possibly find out what it really was he had to express so urgently. The need is implicit in the act and cannot be discussed until the act is accomplished. This is the need that has, most of all, if it is to satisfy itself, to learn the tricks, the sleight-of-hand, which will seduce the public into staying still and listening. Such tricks are, as we have seen, technical. If the writer must, if he needs to, talk about his life out loud in public, he must learn how to fool the eye so that he does not appear to be going on and on about his personal opinions.

If the writer does choose to write about his own life, he will find himself in a position that is probably unique in writing. He will find himself flooded with material that is above all other material fascinating and significant to him and of itself without much interest or meaning to anyone else. To inveigle the reading public into an interest in his life story involves achieving an objectivity that will make him able to select from the intriguing scenes that seem so to crowd it; to be able to think coldly and cunningly about what, in his life, will interest anyone else, and also just why it will interest him and how that interest can be intensified.

In direct opposition to the subjective need for writing autobiography is the apparent need of some people to read about the lives of others with whom they can identify. There is a definite public for the autobiographical story, and I think that it gets part of its satisfaction from the sense of finding problems shared; that we are all in the same boat; that no worry is unique to anyone. I think perhaps this public may be made up of the people I have spoken of in earlier sections who are suspicious of fiction. There appears to be something almost sinister to such people in the idea that a life story can be "all made up." It soothes them to continue with the illusion that what they are reading is absolutely true. I say the illusion that autobiography is true, for it is an axiom with me that it is as impossible to put only factual truth into autobiography as it is impossible to keep it out of fiction. One cannot write down one's memories as they really happened. A, one's memory is not that accurate; and B, the attempt is the surest avenue to achieving a weak effect.

It was with a feeling of achieving freedom that, one day when writing one of my semi-autobiographical stories about a New England girlhood, I realized that I had no moral duty to follow the sequence of events as they really occurred in my childhood. My memories, in other words, were my own. They belonged to me. If I chose to say that I spent the summers in Maine when in reality I spent them in Rhode Island, it was nobody's concern but my own. All anyone could object was that it was not true. Very well; I did not intend it to be true. I intended to have it interesting, and if the summer reads more interestingly about when set in Maine, it is my artistic duty to set it there.

For I am not Churchill or Roosevelt, and what I am writing in autobiographical work is not official; is not history; is not documented. It is entertainment. Furthermore, there is an additional point to be made about the use of phantasy in writing autobiographical stories. Phantasy may in the end produce a result more closely resembling the atmosphere of truth than grim adherence to, say, chronology will. In this connection it is interesting to note that patients in analysis are often advised by analysts that, when writing down their dream in the morning, it does not matter if they have forgotten some of it. They are advised to imagine what it is they *might* have dreamed; for the phantasy will be as important in rendering the needed significance as the dream would have been.

Manes Sperber has this to say about autobiographical writing:

Jean-Jacques Rousseau, author of the most famous "Confessions," wrote, in his first, unpublished draft, "No one can describe the life of a man as well as himself. The real, inner life is known only to himself." Significantly Rousseau had added, "but in describing it, he disguises it . . . he shows himself as he would like to be seen, but not at all as he is."

Thus Rousseau touched on the central problem of all *ego* literature: sincerity and truth. We know today, thanks to the remarkable study, "Jean-Jacques," by Guehenno, that no cynic could have distorted truth more frenetically than this sincerest of men — as Rousseau himself was firmly convinced of being. Astonishing, then, how inefficient a virtue sincerity can be.

André Gide, who, like Rousseau, was educated in a Puritan spirit but lived in a Catholic surrounding, spent sixty years or so on his "Journal," an intimate, soul-searching diary. In contrast to Pepys, Constant and Stendhal, however, he contemplated publishing it very early. He wrote as if in a hermetically sealed house with walls made of magnifying glass so that the public might read every line before the ink was thoroughly dry.

To the first Complete Edition covering fifty years Gide had added, "The image of my mutilated self which I here deliver offers a small hole in place of the heart." This hole has since been filled with the publication — after the death of the great writer — of his "*Et nunc manet in te.*" Nevertheless, it does not change the aspect of the phenomenon which Rousseau characterized as "*faux sincere*" — falsely sincere. Witness the testimony of a most noble and honest man, Roger Martin du Gard, for forty years Gide's intimate, devoted friend. "Never," he wrote, "has an author of 'Confessions' put in so much cunning sincerity in modeling his statue in advance and setting it solidly on a pedestal."

Unquestionably Gide has become a source of great inspiration; the number of writers in France and elsewhere who follow his example will probably grow in the next years and with it a form of *ego* literature, a type of *society* writing in new form. Here, too, virtue and vice, sentiment and attitude, inspiration and incident are the principal substances. Here, too, there is an esoteric side, for in order to grasp all the implications and allusions you yourself must be, at the least, a neighbor to the society of the author. But there is a decisive difference; formerly artifice was considered almost as a quality and often sought for with much naïvete; at present it is abhorred, and sincerity is the thing, if used with considerable cunning, in good, mature style.

No one can deny that there is in our time a strong craving for authenticity. Why, then, shouldn't a confession or testimonial literature take the place of fiction? Cunning or not, sincerity is an indispensable quality. Without it art is always in danger of sinking.

The psychological reasons why this "Open Heart" literature does not bring us nearer to truth are obvious. We shall mention only three of them.

First: in looking in the mirror you don't see yourself as you are; you see a man in a special awkward situation. Of the four characteristic solitudes which man can experience: in face of death, in solitary confinement, in the act of creation and in a looking-glass, the last is the least fertile.

Second: men writing diaries — not à la Pepys and Goncourt, but à la Amiel and Gide — are generally sinful moralists, playing back to themselves a dialogue in which they are accusers and delinquents at the same time. For them guilt sentiment is already a punishment, self-doubt in one's self an inexhaustible source of unavowed pride, remorse an exquisite pain. They are hermits in the midst of society, pilgrims eternally on their way to unreachable holiness, and their diaries self-flagellation.

Third: obsessed by what they want and by what they do not want to be, their knowledge of what they are is, in spite of all soul-searching, rather more fragmentary than other men's. After all, sincerity is the wish, not necessarily the capacity, of discovering and expressing truth. Full-time moralists are rarely good psychologists.

There is also a non-psychological reason for the narrow limits of testamentary literature: differing from fiction, it is unable to solve a fundamental problem of writing, the problem of *time*.

I think we may proceed on the basis that writing autobiographical fiction is nothing if it is not an art. What it attempts to render is *a* truth; not to the past as it once, possibly, existed, but, I believe, to the past as it exists in relation to the present and to the future. This time-space relationship should be created in much the same way as in fiction, for this kind of truth is an artistic, not a literal, one. It can also, of course, be a kind of subjective truth, rendering the by-product of insight into what the author truly was instead of what he thought (as Rousseau thought) he was.

What is possible to the writer of autobiographical fiction, then? Above all it is possible for him to free himself from the solemn sense of duty which bids him stick to history, from the pomposity which persuades him that there is something sacred

— not to be tampered with — about where, when, and how events actually happened to him. He can, in other words, free himself from fact.

I would say, speaking now from a technical point of view, he should avoid the effect that giving events in sequence produces. He should try not to begin at the beginning of his life, in writing about it. Or if he must do that, he should inject some quality into it that will save him from the inevitable impression he will otherwise give of being filled with the wonder of being him.

G. K. Chesterton began *his* autobiography at the beginning, thus: "Bowing down in blind credulity, as is my custom, before mere authority and the tradition of the elders; superstitiously swallowing a story I could not test at the time by experience or private judgment, I am firmly of opinion that I was born on the 29th of May, 1874, on Campden Hill, Kensington, and baptised according to the formularies of the Church of England in the little church of St. George opposite the large Waterworks Tower that dominated that ridge. I do not allege any significance in the relation of the two buildings and I indignantly deny that the church was chosen because it needed the whole water-power of West London to turn me into a Christian."

Profiting by Chesterton's example, we may lay it down that it is wise, in writing autobiography, to be funny if one possibly can about that life which very probably seems far from funny to oneself. A really heart-rending event in my life occurred when I was about sixteen — a boy named Ed Page, whom I worshiped, invited another girl to go to the Middlesex dance with him. I wept, alone and forlorn in the swamp behind our house. Then I went back to the house and took a hot bath, into which I also wept, but which made me feel much better. Writing about this, years later, I saw that it was not tragic but absurd. It is always well to get there first with your laughter, before the public can.

One's life *is* important, it *is* serious and tragic and pathetic and frustrated, right down the line, but if one is going to make it seem in the slightest degree important to that sea of blank faces, a possible public, it has got to be on their terms. They are viewing one coldly from outside. For this reason I would once more recommend that the writer, if possible, instead of relating the events of his life chronologically, in sequence, choose some point on which to stand, as on a springboard, from which he can dive into the past and then return once more. Otherwise he is apt to drown, literarily speaking, in the successive waves of the past, and the reader with him. What he needs is a standard of judgment in the present.

I should like to reprint an autobiographical short story of my own to illustrate what I mean by a standard of judgment.

CHARLOTTE RUSSE

I was looking through a cook book in search of a dessert that would be quick and sweet — in a hurry as usual, because when those great boys come tramping into the house for their supper, they want lots of it, right away, and the dessert had better be a sweet one. Bavarian Cream, I read — but that takes time, stirring over hot water, and so forth. Baked Meringue Custard — not sweet enough. And then my eye fell on the next recipe, Charlotte Russe. I felt a little tremor of joy in my heart at the name, and in spite of the hour, I began reading through the recipe: ". . . combine eggs, salt, and sugar. . . . Cook until mixture coats spoon . . . cool quickly and flavor with vanilla. Fold in the cream which has been stiffly beaten. . . . The mixture should not be stiff enough to mold." Suddenly I felt furious at this heresy to the Charlotte Russe of my childhood, and I let the book shut over my thumb and sat thinking about the way it was.

Nobody knows, nobody can know, how I used to feel about the party dessert that appeared when my father and mother reluctantly, at long intervals during the winter, gave a dinner party. Not stiff enough to mold indeed! It was 'molded in a form with peaks and turrets, so that when it was turned out and stood, an object of beauty, coated with the ladyfingers that had lined the mold, it was like a turreted white castle, like a palace of sparkling dream as I walked round and round it where it was set on the dining-room table to get it out of the hot kitchen. In those days, no icebox could have contained anything so towering, so round, so fragile as the Charlotte Russe.

The table had been enlarged with leaves to make a long oval, and laid with special silver and glass for the approaching rite. For this was the way I thought of those decorous dinner parties, which I never witnessed but only heard from above and clothed in my mind with the veils of perfection. Places were laid for twelve. Instead of the plain glass water tumblers we used every day, at each place was set a high goblet of glass cut in a design of flower garlands, and beside it two wineglasses, one for claret, one for Moselle. The huge damask dinner napkins were folded in the bishop's miter shape and set in the center of the place plates — vast, chilly white, ruby-rimmed. The row of forks extended far to the left of each place. And in the center of all a great epergne of ruby and clear glass was piled with oranges, pomegranates, lady apples, and what my mother used to call deathbed grapes, big and black. On either long side of the centerpiece stood large cut-glass bonbon dishes with covers, on high stems; these held pink and white peppermints from S. S. Pierce's, and, lest the effect be spoiled, I was not allowed to have any until the day after the party. But I did not care; I would rather look than eat. I was allowed, earlier, to help lift the delicate sugary disks from the waxed-paper layers in the white box that had Pierce's gold shield on the cover and lay them gently in the bonbon dishes. There always seemed to be just enough.

On a side table were set out the plates for dessert — white, with a gadroon edge, and a single pink rose painted on each; the rose was now concealed by the thin glass finger bowl, set on a lace doily, flanked by a silver dessert fork and spoon. The finger bowls would not be filled — meaning a bare half inch of water — until just before dinner was served, and then a leaf of lemon verbena would be floated in each, to crush between the fingers at the close of the meal. Also at the close of the meal would be brought out the decanter set — an ebony box inlaid with mother-of-pearl — now decorating the center of the sideboard. When the front and top of the box were turned back on hinges, they disclosed a fairyland of myriad tiny gold-rimmed glasses on stems, set in a gilt framework holding, at the four corners, gold-banded liqueur decanters containing brandy, cherry brandy, apricot brandy, and crème de menthe. The guests would need such marvels, I thought, to sustain them after the high point of the dinner had been passed: the miracle, the ritual destruction of the Charlotte Russe.

Its spires and peaks were now snowy with whipped cream and sparkling with bits of red candied cherries and green angelica. Before the people came, it would be whisked away out into the unheated summer kitchen, where it was too cold to keep it for long. And then they would enter the dining room, I thought — the ladies in their evening gowns with low necks that showed a fascinating crack in front, the gentlemen in their tailcoats and glacial expanses of starched shirt. They would eat, with tablespoons, the cream of tomato soup with the dab of whipped cream floating on it, the oyster soufflé that my mother would have been praying about, the roast, served carved in the kitchen à la russe, with the tiny round balls of potato covered with butter and lemon and parsley, and then it would be time: therefore with angels and archangels they would topple the towers and eat the fragile and delicate substance of the Charlotte Russe. Sometimes there would be a few broken bits of it left the next day, but usually anything left over got consumed in the kitchen; except for once or twice, I never tasted the thing that looked more beautiful, more desirable to me than any food on earth.

All of this I have described represented an enormous outlay of time and energy for my mother, who, if she must have a dinner party, wanted to have it nice. My father categorically resented all activities that took him away from the evenings he liked to spend reading; making dry-point etchings, under the unshaded glare of a blue bulb, with a diamond-point needle; copying the drawings of Watteau in red chalk. I found it almost incredible that they did not enjoy the prospect and the performance of these dinner parties, which so represented the great world to me, but as my father pulled on his evening trousers out in his dressing room he would call in to my mother while, in a camisole, she did her long, wavy, dark-brown hair before the oval mirror in her bedroom, "Well, it can't last more than six hours."

"Six hours!" she would cry, rising to the bait. "If they're asked at seven, it's bad form to stay after half past ten."

My father would wrestle with his boiled shirt as I stood in the open door of the dressing room; his stomach made the dress shirt buckle and bulge. He moved his shoulders uncomfortably under his tailcoat. "I believe in dressing for dinner every night, like the British in India," he said, "but not for a lot of tedious idiots. Well," he called in again to my mother, "a hundred years from now it will all be forgotten."

I would have had my supper earlier, off the kitchen table, while maids hurried and pushed past me, carrying silver that must be polished at the last minute, carrying colanders of dripping vegetables, carrying pots and pans to the soapstone sink from the stove, which was an old-fashioned black coal range with nickel trimming. Maids were always Irish in those days, and they were all named such names as Bridie and Lizzie and Nelly; I remember there was one named Norah whom my mother would get in for dinner parties because she could bone shad.

As I grew older, when the guests arrived I was allowed to come down and speak to them, dressed in my dancing-school black velveteen with the gold moire sash run through slots. I took the hand of each ravishing lady, each indulgent gentleman, in turn, kicking the floor behind me with one toe in lieu of a curtsy. The room smelled of the fresh roses the ladies wore tucked in their tulle fichus, and of the things the gentlemen put on their hair. They all looked, to me, excited and aware of the thrilling events before them — the unfolding of those napkins, the shattering of that Charlotte Russe; apotheosized, and not at all like the torpid people I knew as the parents of my school friends, reading the Sunday paper on a late-winter morning. Everyone looked stimulated, including my parents; but a little canker of sorrow told me that with them it was not sincere; they were not really thrilled, but bored, and wishing the dinner party were over. In those days, at least in our house, no one was given anything to drink before dinner, so I only stayed down for a few minutes. Bridie would come to the door: "Dinner is served, mum" — and there began the bustle and chattering confusion of going in to dinner. I would climb the stairs to my own room. That was the last I saw of the dinner party; it was never the custom in our house, as I have read it is in some houses, for the child to come down for dessert.

When I was in bed, I would lie still, with the window open to the dark, snowy winter night, and let my feelings soar. I could faintly hear the hum of conversation in the dining room underneath me; when the door between the dining room and the kitchen was opened, a burst of laughter would float up the back stairs. The people at the dinner party were Olympian, seated around a Parnassian table loaded with the fare of gods. I could hear the footsteps of the maids, hurrying over the wooden floor of the kitchen to wait upon them. They drank from crystal goblets; their napkins were vast, satiny; their jokes were, surely, magnificent and immortal. And in the center of it all was, for me, the Charlotte Russe, borne into the dining room at the last by careful hands, inviolate, and then broken into with silver serving fork and spoon. I could see it happening — that perfection of whipped cream, cherries, and angelica, its towers fallen. Much as I loved the Charlotte Russe, I took pleasure in thinking of their shattering it. And when I in my turn became grown-up — enormous, invulnerable — I, too, would sit at dinner parties, be passed exquisite, trembling confections, break into them with fork and spoon without even looking, my head turned as I exchanged ineffable witticisms with the gentleman beside me.

I don't need to say that this flood of recollection that came on me as I sat in the kitchen with the cook book in my lap made me late with everything for the rest of the afternoon. The boys came in before I was half ready with their supper, and no dessert made. I can't imagine what led me to waste so much time, because actually there's nothing I want to do less than unpack all that china and glass that's been in this attic ever since the old house was broken up. And as for making a great, elaborate, extravagant dessert, I haven't the time or energy. I'm tired when I get the dishes done at night, and glad to follow my husband into the living room and read the evening paper. He's finished with it by that time, and the boys are upstairs doing their homework, and we can be quiet and peaceful in the family circle, hoping to goodness nobody drops in.

At the risk of sounding sententious, I should like to point out that in writing this piece I was not interested in conveying any great truths about how people gave dinner parties in those days. As a matter of fact, as my mother will testify, her dinners weren't much like that. Nobody was more surprised than she when "Charlotte Russe" came out. "That's the first I knew we had vast satiny napkins," she remarked.

The truth I *was* interested in expressing — and this is where I may sound sententious — is a truth about what being grown up is: what it seems like when you are looking forward to being grown up, and what it is like when you actually get there.

The other angle of the time-space problem that has to be dealt with in writing autobiographically is the angle that the future represents. The reader can, after all, read on the jacket what has really become of the author — whether he is living in New York or California, whether he is married or single, alive or dead. There is in short no mystery, no suspense, about the outcome of autobiographical writing. Therefore the author has to create some. I would say that the problem of creating suspense in autobiographical writing is the most difficult of all. A comparison may here be made with the movies, where we all know the heroine won't be killed, simply because it's Audrey Hepburn, but where we nevertheless can get all wrought up because the situations into which she is put are such we recognize the danger inherent in them and respond, as humans, with terror. The reader of the book jacket knows what really happened to the author, but it is possible to get him so wrought up about the author's narrow squeezes in life that for a time his knowledge of literal reality is suspended.

I do not mean by this that a writer should fill his autobiographical writing with actual situations of danger so that the reader forgets what he read on the jacket about his being a garage mechanic in Rocky Mount, North Carolina, and fears for his death by earthquake. I mean a psychological balance which must be struck between past, present, and future. The present is where the writer should, I believe, stand, as narrator of what he has to say; the past is what he is narrating; the future should be kept a sort of live mystery, so that the reader is kept wondering how what the writer is saying of the past will determine the nature of the future. What is to come of all this? We must continually wonder. Thus, in the famous autobiographies, we continually wonder about the progress of Saint-Simon's position at court; we fear for the results of Boswell's gargantuan appetite for wenching; we worry about the consequences of his vice, in the *Confessions* of Gide. What I would suggest is that the choice of material for autobiographical writing — for autobiography must be quite as selective in its own way as fiction — be determined by the potentialities of that material for future development. There is no point in writing about your sixth birthday party unless something came of it, by, perhaps, your having met your dearest friend of life on that occasion.

So-called confessional writing can be seductive for this reason, of course. But I would like to suggest that the author doesn't have to give away any of the juicier secrets of his private life in order to continue to hold the reader's attention. What is needed is continuity; the sense of life. The reader should stand, with the author, on that precarious springboard of the present. Below them lies the sea, or past. Above them reaches the sky, which is the limitless future. A recognition of them all is needed to give the reader that sense of life. Only so can the past, I believe, be redeemed from the sense of death. I hope that in "Charlotte Russe" I managed during most of it to convey the impression that the giving of formal dinner parties is my idea of the ultimate in bliss. I hope that the acceptance, at the end, of the reality of being grown up and tired — feeling, in short, much like my own parents about making an effort — came as a shock and a surprise. I hope this ending had a kind of reality, or life.

But I would like to give a word of caution against being led into the caressing of dead objects. It is wise not to dwell with nostalgia upon the cocker spaniel which was given you on your twelfth Christmas, unless he can be given a living place in your development; unless the reader can see perhaps that he was the reason for your having walked down that long dark path through the woods you had never dared before, and discovered the clearing at the end where wildflowers grew and where ever afterwards you used to bring your homework as to a secret garden; where, in turn, you first read the book that gave you your life's interest in zoology. It is wise, in short, not to bring up and caress dead objects unless you can inject into them a living value, and I am afraid this means a symbolical value.

But in defense of the symbol I might add that symbols really are what convey us out of the past into the future, as in a wedding-ring, an heirloom, a keepsake, a letter, a watch charm, a medal. All these objects represent something more than what they are. They represent the giver of them, or the owner of them, or the sender or maker of them. They convey meaning — which is what makes life worth while — from the past into the future.

I think that at its best the art of writing autobiographically can be such a conveyer of life. Out of what is past it selects what is of value and transfers it into the future, over and across the present. It is like an heirloom with vital associations, a keepsake of feeling, a club cup shared with other members. The trick is to make the reader of one's book feel like a member. This means that one must, in such writing, select material that will give the reader a feeling of participation, of identification. That this is a trick has been demonstrated to me over and over again by the nature of the letters I get about my semi-autobiographical writing.

Again and again such a letter will begin by saying, "I loved your stories about your childhood — it was exactly like mine." It then goes on to relate the writer's own reminiscences, which are not slightly different from mine, but diametrically different. Instead of being an only child, she was one of eight. Instead of summering at the seashore, she went to the mountains. Instead of going to a Boston day school, she was sent away — far, far away — to school, perhaps in Switzerland. Sometimes after reading such a letter I wonder what possible likeness the sender felt with my childhood.

I think it is because people do like to get together and have a good talk about their youths. Nobody listens to anybody else, except to be reminded of something that happened to *him* when he was ten. I have come to believe that this is a basic impulse. For the writer of autobiography it means something important: that there is something in readers which can be reached; an instinct to share memories, a desire to compare notes on living. Feeling for the past speaks to feeling for the past. Nobody, it is true, cares about Miss Hale's opinions; what people care about is that we *all* have opinions about life.

Therefore I think I am right if I say that what the writer should try to do if he writes about his life is to evoke; to awaken an echo in other lives; to arouse a consciousness where perhaps formerly there was none. Memory of the past appears to be an unevenly distributed gift. People without much of it love to have what they do have awakened. What such people as this will look for in a book about one's life is not its unusual events — although one must probably include them too — but its quality of universality, its offering a seat to them in that same boat we are all in.

A book is not really a front porch on which writer and reader can sit down and rock together. The writer must always be the prestidigitator, and the reader must always be the one who is taken in by the tricks (or not taken in by the tricks). However, in writing about his own life the writer has a definite instinct to appeal to. He is trying all the while to make it seem as if we *were* all sitting on some cosmic front porch together, rocking, exchanging long, gratifying accounts of our happy or unhappy lives. At any moment, the writer is trying to make it seem, the reader can break in upon the writer's stream of discourse, crying, "Why, that's just the way it was with me!"

TWELVE

How to Keep from Writing

AFTER so much about writing, it might not be amiss to say a word about not-writing; about the state that almost all writers get into at times, when they either can't write at all — have no ideas, perhaps — or can't write what they want to, at least in the way they want to. It is an all-too-familiar state to writers, and it might possibly prove as helpful to discuss some of the reasons for such a state, and some of the cures for it, as to talk solely about when one is in the groove.

Possibly the most constructive and the most successful approach to these states is summed up in the phrase "lying fallow." Just as a field cannot be planted and harvested year after year without an occasional off year, which adds immeasurably in the end to its eventual yield, a mind cannot go on and on creating and producing in the same groove, or, shall we say, rut. Or rather, it *can* go on doing just that, but with results which are not creative at all, but destructive; tragic.

What is needed, in a mind as in a field, is change — change of crop, change of cycle. But while you can plant alfalfa or kudzu in a field to refresh it and make it newly fertile, a mind must produce its own changes, out of the same depths which sent up the created works. For we are not discussing the kind of change which is meant by a trip abroad, or by a new hat, but the profounder change which will result in a new creation. It is the kind of change that is most clearly recognized when it is not forthcoming.

Readers used to say of J. P. Marquand's work, for years, "Why does he keep writing the same story over and over? Why doesn't he change sometimes?" Well, why didn't he? The theme that Marquand repeated so often was of the sensitive young man with an inferiority complex, out in the hard-boiled callous world of modern materialistic values, and he repeated it so often that we may feel justified in assuming that this was something he needed badly to say. It was, in fact (although dressed in a variety of different costumes), Marquand's own psychological dilemma, a dilemma he explained to himself and to the world so often that we must also assume that he himself needed to grasp this idea and understand it, very badly indeed. We might also assume that a maturer Marquand might have replied, finally, to the self that kept sending him this message, something like, "Yes, I get it. I see that, thank God, I'm no longer a young man with any reason to feel inferior, I'm a grown man with great talent and considerable powers." Then, just possibly, we might assume that he could go on from there whenever the fresh theme, the fresh angle of the life problem every man faces till the day he dies, arose to capture his imagination. But this never happened. Marquand never dealt with the problem that kept presenting itself in his fiction, or accepted it in any such way as would settle it and allow him to pass on to the next thing.

He did experience one great change earlier, which came when he moved away from the writing of trivial fiction to the first of the more committed books that were to introduce this life problem which from then on consumed his attention. To the reader looking on, it seems tragic that Marquand was never able to see that a writer, in writing his best, is always communicating not only with the world but with himself. He is telling a tale not only to the world but to himself; a tale disguised, it is true (as when a child puts his wrath into a story of a wicked king who goes around killing everybody), but a tale *somebody* is supposed to hear, and understand, and to do something about. It is a cry for help. Great art is like love, in that it does not move only out, or only in, but both out and in, at once. It has a meaning for the world, and a meaning for its own creator. But the majority of writers are unaware that their products reflect their own psychological status, or that there is anything for them to gain from their works in addition to skill, money, and prestige. I don't mean that art is a psychological exercise. I mean that the problem engaging the mind is the problem of the self, and art solves the problem.

The unawareness of this has something to do, I think, with the assumption everywhere prevalent today that productivity is good and non-productivity is bad. As Aldous Huxley points out, it is the West's concept that contemplation is only a means to action. Action is everywhere the acknowledged desideratum. But the trouble with continuous, uninterrupted productivity is that it is hermetically sealed off from change. There is no time to reflect, in a career which demands ceaseless productivity; and without reflection there can be no change, no time to see the "slow miracles of thought take shape through patience into grace."

Poor Sinclair Lewis watched as though aghast as his novels became weaker in quality while he churned out one after another of them. His self-respect was based upon his being a writer, a successful one and a good one. He had to keep writing to support his self-respect, never pausing except for alcoholic excursions up the river, of which the less said the better. His novels changed, all right; they deteriorated while he sat helpless over the typewriter, unable to stop what was happening. He never seems to have heard that warning which, in a special writer's sense, might be called "Stop, Look, Listen." Stop to look at what you are doing, and listen to what it is trying to say, to tell, to reveal about itself. If Lewis could have reread his great novels — *Babbitt, Arrowsmith,* and *Main Street* — not only to admire what he had done but to hear what he was trying to say to himself, he might, like Marquand if he had done that, have learned something to free him to go on to something different and better still.

It has often been remarked in literary criticism that the reason first novels are so often their writers' best work is that those first novels draw upon a whole childhood full of brooding, of reflection, of wandering in the woods, of private anguish and secret delight. *Not,* you will notice, of hectic activity. Of melancholy, rather; of inertia. Yet it has been less often remarked that when comparable periods of inertia strike an adult writer, he tends to flee them with cries of horror, terming them periods of depression or else of "running dry."

What if he is not running dry at all? What if his organism

is doing its best to present him, through what we earlier called lying fallow, a time of restocking his pond, of letting the laurels he has cut down grow up again? What if, by rejecting what is happening to him (and will happen to him anyway whether he likes it or not), he is turning away from an opportunity to feel, smell, touch, and hear life in the pristine state he experienced it in as a child — not as a writer but as a human being? What if he is losing his opportunity to become a better writer? Professionalism is sometimes a curse to a writer, setting up salability and efficiency as the only criteria of value. It seems to me that true creativity knows its own value, and seeks to publish itself as a natural sequence. One might say that productivity, for a writer, represents doing in the cycle of creation, and lying fallow represents the being and becoming in it.

Looked at in this sense, these periods of non-productivity which come to every writer may be seen as not sterile but creative, in a different sense from the periods of his greatest production. What is involved is the relation between art and life. Life, of course, feeds art, gives grist to its mill, and art in turn can feed life, supplying the writer with answers to his problems and the key to further development. This movement in to art and then out again to real life has the motion — wave-like, flowing, non-repetitive — that, it seems to me, is characteristic of all real thought. It is productivity in a straight, unbroken line; it is unceasing hammering on the same note; it is the blind drive to action and the flight from contemplation that seem to me to be against life. In other words, the cure (if we ought to call it that) for periods of not-writing is not to rail against non-productivity, or compulsively to repeat old formulas that have worked in the past. It is an open-minded receptivity to whatever will be sent. It is an acceptance of the essential place lying fallow has in the cycle of creativity. The great thing for the writer is to have faith that he will write again. If he keeps his wits about him and looks and listens acutely enough, he may even write better.

F. Scott Fitzgerald was a writer who in the body of his work displays an astonishing capacity to change and develop. He was one that seemed able to learn from his mistakes and from the account of himself embodied in his fiction and go on to new things.

Otto Friedrich, in an article on Fitzgerald, comments on the childish and boring preoccupation with money and glamor which looms so large in Fitzgerald's early successes *This Side of Paradise* and *The Beautiful and Damned*. Their characters, Friedrich says, are "not essentially damned, but damned drones, who would never have had a moment's anxiety if only some kind fate had supported them in the style to which they were accustomed. Even such clichés would have fitted them to perfection." If they had not been the novelty that they in fact were in those days, it is doubtful whether these two books would have commanded much attention. If they had not been followed by the great work by which they in fact were followed, it is doubtful whether they would be remembered today.

But they were. They were written by a man whose talent was far from that swimming-pool with a limited capacity Fitzgerald himself fancied energy to be. Instead, this talent was like a spring, a spring which could turn and twist, find new outlets and keep flowing, whether underground or over it. The novels we have mentioned, with their shoddy glamor and absurd characters, were followed by *The Great Gatsby*, one of the most nearly perfect novels of our time; and in the character of Jay Gatsby we are privileged to see the artist portray, satirize, and totally understand that worship of money which the same artist was a sucker for in his first two novels.

Somewhere in between he has learned much. He has changed. It is hard to realize that the great book is by the same man who wrote the silly ones. Where did Fitzgerald's change of outlook come from? — for this was a real change. In the writer it took place in, it represents a diametrical reversal from that earlier self of which he could say, "I worked for money to share the mobility of the rich and the grace that some of them brought into their lives."

This change in Fitzgerald has been traced to a succession of failures that came to him after his first startling triumph. One might add at this point that it is not success which tends to produce change in a writer, but, on the contrary, produces more of the same. It is failure that makes a man think; that makes him stop, look, and listen. Why have I failed? a man will ask himself; and it is the intelligent response to this question that results in real changes.

In Toynbee's historical work he speaks again and again of the dynamic mechanisms which he terms withdrawal and return, and challenge and response; by which, he demonstrates, all the great changes of history have been made possible. In its simplest form this basic activity may be seen when a man, confronted with a decision to make about something out in the world, withdraws from it, if only momentarily, into himself to make up his mind, and then emerges, his choice made. I know a man who almost visibly climbs down into a hole to make a decision; then you can see him peeping up out of it again when he has decided what he is going to do.

Failure is such a confrontation — for failure is a fact, and what is the author of the failure going to do about it? He must climb into some sort of hole. He must in fact *construct* for himself a nice hole, to climb down into before he can make any intelligent move to correct the situation. The hole that the writer climbs down into is, I think, much the same hole that he climbs into in order to write; but on the type of occasion we are discussing he climbs into it, not to imagine another story, but to imagine a kind of self that could be capable of writing another kind of story.

The blows Fitzgerald sustained after the first flush of his success are generally thought to be the failure of his only play, *The Vegetable*; his association with the brilliant and misogynistic Ring Lardner, whose own failure in the face of a great talent saddened and possibly frightened Fitzgerald; and the first signs of serious instability in his wife Zelda, displayed in her affair with a French aviator on the Riviera.

The kind of change that is needed to meet the challenge of defeat is always a change in basic philosophy. The philosophy that is expressed in *This Side of Paradise* and *The Beautiful and Damned* was manifestly inadequate to support or deal with any blows from life whatsoever. Yet one can only too well imagine a lesser writer going on and on, blindly; unable to grasp that what once had proved successful should not continue to be so, like the child who has made its elders laugh once and so keeps repeating the same silly remark. It might be objected here that Fitzgerald's failures were in his life, not his work; but in fact how is one to distinguish between failure in the work and failure in the life? In Fitzgerald the work, up to that time, failed to support the life, up to that time. A change was required.

This is not the moment to go off into literary criticism, since what I am trying to do here is discuss the mechanism by which change is accomplished in a writer and his work. Yet I think it essential to our purpose to quote a little more of the Friedrich essay on Fitzgerald, in which he says of the change that happened that "the most important element in the greatness of *The Great Gatsby* — and a direct result of his personal evolution — was that Fitzgerald finally tried to tell the truth. Instead of attempting to assume the sham gentility and the mainly imaginary problems of The Ivy Leaguer, he returned to the shabby Western world, for the character of James Gatz of North Dakota.

"Fitzgerald himself said, 'Gatsby started out as one man I knew and then changed into myself.' Fitzgerald's part in Gatsby represented the authenticity of self-knowledge he would never admit in his earlier portraits of playboys. At the end of *The Great Gatsby*, the protagonist, Garraway, can shout across the lawn to Gatsby, 'They [the rich playboys] are a rotten crowd. You're worth the whole bunch put together.' For Fitzgerald, this was not only a judgment, but an explosion of hatred against the things he had once admired. Symbolically, he is accusing the rich of murdering him." (Or, one might add, his glamor self of murdering his real self.)

I have quoted thus extensively with the purpose of making another point about change of philosophy in a writer and his work: that a change, to be a change, is always in the direction of truth. Not, I hasten to say, literal truth — Jay Gatsby is nothing like the Francis Scott Key Fitzgerald who grew up in St. Paul, Minnesota — but in the direction of a deeper truth. We might oversimplify and say that it was Fitzgerald's seeing through the illusion of money and glamor, to a balanced truth about them, which both made *The Great Gatsby* a great book and Fitzgerald the writer who could write it. This is oversimplifying, because to embrace the pious clichés is of itself of no value to a writer. It is a new seeing that is called for. William James says that the simplest basic experience of mysticism is that moment when one suddenly realizes a new meaning for an adage, when one is visited by its new meaning as by a dawn. Just so, the kind of experience Fitzgerald had in regard to some of his earlier illusions must have been of a profound and emotional kind — a real change; a conversion.

A change again took place in Fitzgerald in order to make him the writer who could produce *Tender Is the Night*. Here the change was less golden. The book was a partial failure, not because it wasn't a complete popular success, but because it was not the virtuoso performance *Gatsby* was. But it is a great book. Friedrich points out that if *Gatsby* was the result of doubts, cracks, and anxieties, *Tender Is the Night* emerged from upheavals that would have silenced a lesser writer. Zelda's mental breakdown and his own ruined health from alcoholism would have been enough to wreck any book. Yet the book was not wrecked. It is wonderful. It is, above all, a change. Once more Fitzgerald was able to learn from the past and change in relation to the future, by acting differently in the present. *Tender Is the Night* represents Fitzgerald's insight into the fraud of his own dream of success.

The collection of essays Fitzgerald wrote for *Esquire*, published posthumously under the title *The Crack-Up,* constitutes one of the most searching and ruthless self-examinations any writer can ever have put himself to. A young man who wants to be a writer said to me lately that he had left Harvard after his sophomore year because Harvard has no value; because the only good he could get out of it would be its degree, for the purpose of getting a job; and because all real education, he said, has to be self-won, and so Harvard is a waste of time. I said I agreed. Education *is* self-won, I said. But, I added, you've got to have the stamina to go to all your own classes, and you've got to be willing to give yourself all those examinations. He thought I was sneering at him, but I wasn't. The realest kind of education does include self-examinations.

To read *The Crack-Up* is to see what it is to examine yourself, as for a Ph.D. oral on life, time, love, and illusion. I suspect that Fitzgerald the examining board may have flunked Fitzgerald the candidate, but, reading the essays, we today may pass him. I don't think he spared himself a thing within the framework of the larger illusion in which of course he still did operate. For the examiners are subject to the same errors that the candidate is judged on. Fitzgerald's grand illusion, of course — an indissoluble one — was alcohol.

Friedrich says that as reflected in these essays, Fitzgerald's breakdown — for it was his physical and emotional collapse which he was writing about — seems, instead of the disintegration of reality that marks the usual crackup, like an awakening from unreality. It seems like the awakening from a once-pleasant dream that had become a nightmare. Fitzgerald's social life had become that of the middle-aged drunk. His wife was hopelessly insane. He himself was emotionally atrophied. It was a state comparable to, but more severe than, Sinclair Lewis's condition when he was writing progressively worse and worse.

However, Fitzgerald could still change. He began writing *The Last Tycoon*, which is not like anything else in his work. I myself don't think it is the marvel some critics have blown it up into, but I could be wrong; it was never anywhere near finished. My point is that it was a new departure, a change, at a time when another writer might either have quit or written a real lemon. Fitzgerald had more in him than he ever gave himself credit for. His changes were all in the direction of truth and away from illusion. But the strongest illusion of all was what he sought in alcohol, which had by this time become a physical necessity. In other words, it too was true. Instead of illusion vanishing before the light of truth, this particular illusion had turned into another, and a dark, truth.

Change, then, we have seen to be essential if the writer is to continue fertile and productive. And we have seen that change cannot, on the face of it, occur if one persistently goes on doing the same thing over and over. The reason so many people — and not only writers — are afraid of change is because change feels so destructive. In fact, change is destructive, in that, through it, the old is done away with. It is my theory that perhaps the reason writers are so often frightened of their seemingly unproductive periods is that during them phantasies of destruction in the form of melancholy and depression so often occur. But it is these very phantoms that they must turn to account.

Let us agree that change cannot occur in the writer in the midst of his productivity. Yeats says somewhere in his *Autobiography*: "A man going at full speed has neither heart nor head." Let us agree that his periods of non-productivity (which are certainly a fact and might as well be accepted as such) are, in addition, potentially valuable. They are breeders of new material, new philosophy, new insight and understanding. How should a writer behave when he is dumped down into that state which a novelist friend of mine calls "in the soup"? What must he do when he further withdraws into fallowness from that other, earlier withdrawal from life which is art itself?

For a writer, to think about his work is the same thing as to think about himself, since his work is himself, expressed in fictional terms. I am fond of that sentence I quoted in an earlier section which expresses this: "Literature is the guile some personalities develop in disguising their deeper emotions." I might say that in that earlier withdrawal from full participation in life which the adoption of art as a way of life represents, it was the very painfulness of thinking about the self at all, the impossibility of facing one's illusions, that led one to couch them in fictional (that is to say disguised) form. For it is oneself that one disguises the deeper emotions from, as well as other people. Only when this armor is once achieved can one think constructively about one's work in the kind of way Fitzgerald did; is one able to see through the illusions that have hampered, not only the work, as Fitzgerald's early work was hampered, but the mind that conceived and wrote them.

In other words, writing is one way of dealing with the deeper moral problems of life. This kind of way needs overhauling from time to time if it is to remain adequate to new tasks. Change is required to fit the tool to the task, and change is accomplished, in part, by self-examination and reflection.

The problem, then, for the writer, is how to think constructively about his work and, through it, about himself. If change had not been required, he would never have fallen into the soup in the first place. It is analogous to the old concept of inertia, by which a ball continues to roll indefinitely unless something opposes it. The writer, rolling along, has been opposed by something. Something has occurred to stop him. This is the challenge; what is to be the response?

In the first place, it is a truism to say that the way to start thinking constructively about oneself is to avoid the subject. As in listening to music, too rigid attention is fatal. A simple example of this would be the kind of occasion when one tries to remember a name and can't. Yet, when one relaxes and makes no special mental effort, the name comes swimming into consciousness. Similarly, what the writer is looking for, in the soup, is a new standard of judgment about his work, a new attitude. He is looking for a change. He doesn't even know what the change ought to be.

He should forget it. Or rather, he should first remember that what he is looking for is a new standard and a new attitude, and *then* forget it. I don't think he can try to find it. I think it must come to him. I think he must let it — whatever it may be — suggest itself to him at odd moments, around the crack of a door, through a cranny in a stone wall; shocking him, surprising him. I have heard writers in this pickle say that it helps to read the work of other writers whom they most admire. I have found myself turning in such a case to such writers as Rilke, Proust, Katherine Mansfield, in her letters and journals, to Tolstoi's short stories. But every writer will have his own tuning fork to set the key for his own reflections.

He might take walks, if he likes to take walks. He might, if he is free to, do things he liked to do when he was a child — paint, perhaps; garden, play the piano, or whatever. He might do these remembering all the time that they are only a means of quieting the mind in order to admit the entrance into it of the unknown thing he lacks — the essential thing that must come from within.

In short, the writer might relax; at the same time that he is watchful like a wise virgin at midnight. What does him the most harm, I believe, is getting nerved up at such a time and thinking that he cannot write any more, ever, because he cannot write now. It may be that what he needs is simply to moon, as he mooned as a child. (Look at what came of that.)

If the writer desires at the same time to make motions like a writer, he might engage himself in listening to other people talking, instead of talking so much himself. He might listen for their locutions and their accents, their enunciations and their mannerisms. He might listen to the rhythms of silence and the rhythms of locomotion. When he has learned them, they may later come in handy, the way the things he used to listen to as a child have come in handy. He might brood over what he sees and hears, too. He might wonder why people act the way they do. He might write down his dreams in the morning and then brood about why he should have dreamed them in the first place.

It is wise for him to listen. For he is here — in the soup — to learn. People are only too eager to find someone who will listen to the stories of their sad, dramatic, or strange lives. He might listen to them. He might pay attention to why a woman of fifty, able and self-reliant, should weep with bitter self-recrimination when her mother of eighty dies. Or why a man who has finally, after a battle, won a divorce from a wife he loathes and married a nice and charming young girl, should go all to pieces when the news reaches him that wife number one has shot herself. Or why a woman whose main interest in life, so she claims, is humanity, should never hear anything her husband says unless he repeats it, so that he has formed a habit of saying everything twice over automatically.

The writer might also take notes, if he likes to take notes, on this sort of tiny observation. He might keep a journal, perhaps, in which to examine his artistic conscience — unfashionable as such journals are today. But he should not, above all, keep reminding himself that he is unable to write. Rather, he might make himself a promise that he *won't* write, not until something has happened to make him feel differently about his work, until he can see life and work a new way.

However, Nature's edges never come together into a neat join. They always overlap. There may come a time when the writer needs to nudge himself into trying to write again and to see if perhaps things have changed inside himself when he was not looking, without his realizing it. This sometimes does happen. When he is writing again he will know if it is so. After all, no one is going to put up a flag for him saying The Fleet Is In. Since what is changing is the writer himself, he may not know at first that he is any different.

Years ago I read a prescription for stimulating the flow of writing which still seems to me valuable. It is to go to the typewriter on first getting up in the morning, without speaking to anyone, and writing for half an hour, anything that comes to mind. Even if the results seem, read, and are like twaddle, the real idea is to let the contents of the mind, in a semi-conscious state, flow. This is purely an exercise, and the results should not be kept. It might also prove refreshing not to think of every single thing produced as professional, but to write like a child, for pleasure and for self-expression.

Underneath all this, of course, remains the hard necessity for self-examination. The writer might pick the subject of his semi-conscious writing with some care, bearing this in mind. He might pick the dream of last night to analyze as if it were fiction. Or he might write about what most enrages him in the work of some other author, and then ponder why it should so enrage him. Or about what he most admires and envies in another author, and ponder *that*. The thing for him is to use the relaxed state to trap what he needs to know about himself; about why he has failed; about what he lacks. If he is nerved up and out gunning for what is the matter, he is far less likely to sight the quarry. But if he pretends he is not really looking very hard, he may just suddenly see what it is he is looking for, standing like a golden-brown deer in a clearing in the deep pine woods.

The first thing that I have been trying to say is that the writer should not worry if he cannot write. He will. And the other thing I am trying to say is, opportunity is hidden in his period of non-productivity — the opportunity for reflection, the opportunity for change. Change for a writer is, as we have seen, the progressive facing of the truth. It is a loosening of the bonds that have tied him to illusion. Anyone who is really a writer is going to keep on being a writer. He always was, he always will be. It is the people who were not really writers who drop out — much to their own and other people's advantage. But if the writer is going to become a better writer, he has got to be ready, willing, and waiting for his chance to change.

At this point I, like the old crone in fairy tales who has led the adventurous hero to the edge of the forest, must leave the writer. He must go into the forest alone. I can't even tell him what it is that he is in search of. But it ought to be a help, when he finds himself alone under those dark cathedral pines, to realize that he is, at least, in search of *something*. And, like the old crone, I can also give him a parting word of counsel: Fear not.

{ *THIRTEEN* }

❦

Poetry: The Other Side of the Cove

THE PRINCIPAL worry of worriers about the state of poetry (and I, not content with worrying the short story, am one of them) is that matter of communication. My poet friends *will* get to talking about whether the poets are communicating, and with whom, and if not why not; and about whether the public is being communicated *with*, and by what poets, and if so why so. All this talk seems to be posited upon the assumption that, to put it bluntly, the public is the enemy. Perhaps it is. So is Russia the enemy, and so do we need to communicate with it. John Hall Wheelock told me of a young poet who had submitted a book of verse for publication with the assurance that it was "reader-proof," which raises the fascinating speculation that perhaps the poet does not want to hold summit conferences with the public. In any case, last summer at our place on Cape Ann, I heard my mother, who is not a writer but a painter, say something impatient which seemed to me to hit one of the nails of communication on the head.

Our house there is on a granite hill, looking across a small,

cuplike blue cove to a point of land which is pink where the
sun falls on its solid rock, and beyond it to Ipswich Bay. We
bathe off sun-warmed glacial boulders that rim the cove. To the
left, the land at the end of the cove rises — a slope where
locust trees grow thickly, their bark as dry and white as bones.
Generations of children have called it the magic or the fairy
wood. To the right, outside the cove's mouth, the ocean
stretches northeast without a break between us and Portugal. If
one lets the eye slide back, southward, along the horizon,
Mount Agamenticus in Maine can, on a clear day, be seen. Still
farther along, the shapes of Newburyport and then of Ipswich
are visible, the silhouettes of their houses and trees tiny and
accurate as toy model villages beyond the green-streaked, dark-
blue bay.

But last summer none of this was seen by anybody much,
for we chanced to be visited by an influx of intellectuals. (I
thought of Muriel Draper, years ago, when Gilbert Seldes and
Lincoln Kirstein entered the room, setting up the cry, "Hurrah!
The intellectuals are coming!") They would walk down the
white pebbly road, heads bowed in thought. They sat hunched
on the rocks, not noticing the minute red spiders that run
from one crack in the granite to another. When they swam,
they wore goggles, with snorkels to breathe through, staring
down, down into dark waters where lobsters hitch themselves
along like green thoughts through a desert mind. Sometimes
they encased themselves in black or red rubber suits and
totally immersed themselves in that element which, to the
psychiatrist, symbolizes the unconscious. They would read
books as they sat there in the joyous mornings, or even while
they took walks. As they sat in bathing suits on the rocks they

would sometimes converse — for some of them were poets — about this matter of communication: How the poet is not making himself heard; how no one listens; how the poet's language is getting lost. It was on one of the latter occasions that my mother, who had been growing more and more exasperated at not having the ravishments of her favorite spot on earth appreciated or, for that matter, viewed, remarked tartly, "I don't see how you can communicate with anybody if you won't even look at anything."

There was a short silence. Then the conversation turned politely to painting. "You simply *live* through your eyes, don't you?" a young woman said sympathetically to my mother. "I've noticed the way you painters keep saying 'Look at that. . . . Look at that.' . . . all the time." It seemed to be the sense of the meeting that a red herring of visual arts had been dragged across the trail of the problem of communication in poetry. But when, afterwards, I found myself thinking over my mother's exclamation, I wondered if the young woman, who is a brilliant and frequently obscure writer, remembered it too. (In this young woman's case, what happens is that readers think she is bitter about life, when what she is really feeling is wounded. She means one thing, they get another. "What can I do about it if they take it wrong?" she said to me once.)

The fact is that it is easiest to hear what is said when one is being directly addressed. I am speaking from the analogy which everywhere obtains between the postures of real life and the postures of art. It is not a question of yelling. It is a question of regarding the object one would address. The voice, then, does the rest. This is the secret of the lecturer who fixes his eye on the fat woman in the back row and talks exclusively to her. Many poets and persons — and I have come to suspect that they constitute a definite type — by nature, perhaps, tend to avert their eyes, contemplate their visible or invisible navels, and mumble. One angelic intellectual I know is likely to speak to me as if I existed underneath his belt buckle. When I in turn keep saying "What? . . . What? . . ." he seems wounded, offended, and even somewhat surprised that I have popped up (so deaf and stupid) in the outer world.

On the other hand, miracles of communication can be effected when a speaker speaks for, to, and with a hearer. On those same pink granite rocks at Cape Ann I once sat, in bathing suits, with a young man from Georgia. Let it be said that he had never been in New England before, loathed children, and that his voice was gentle to the point of inaudibility. Across the cove rise the steep cliffs of the point, for some hundred feet up to a crown of coarse grass and sassafras trees. As the young man and I sat facing them, we saw three small, skinny boys begin to scale the cliffs, zigzagging along the diagonal seams in the rock and clinging on somehow with their fingers. "They'll be killed!" I exclaimed. "They're bound to fall!" The young man glanced briefly at me. Then, seeing his duty, he cupped his hands around his mouth. "Kids, *oh* kids!" he called, not very loud. "Come down yere off those rocks or I'll snatch you baldheaded, hear?"

The children paused and appeared to confer. Then they started backing down the way they had come, which wasn't far. As New England children, they were unlikely to have heard the locutions my friend employed, but his meaning conveyed itself perfectly. He was using, of course, the vocative case (which I am old enough to remember memorizing). Is it mere chance, I wonder, that the vocative case is today dropped from the declensions of Latin and Greek nouns in schools? Grammars define the vocative case as "the form of direct address," and what I am suggesting here is that anything — a poem or a command — is more likely to be heard if it is directly addressed to something which is regarded. Much poetry, past and present, seems not addressed to anybody, unless it is to the poet's conscious self. Perhaps there is a poetry which is meant to be to, for, and with the self, and another poetry which is addressed to somebody else or to something other, if only the reader. This latter poetry can not only speak *of* the enemy but would be capable, I should think, of raising its voice to cry into the void, O enemy! Interestingly enough, there is no vocative case for the noun "self."

In the past poets were continually using the vocative. Not only did the poet address his coy mistress, the western wind, Helen, Lucasta, the shrine of his dead saint, the laurels and myrtles, the immortal Bird, the vain deluding joys, merchildren, Maud, death, or time itself, but he also nearly always buttonholed an unnamed reader and, in at least the tones of direct address, told him of the building that had gone forward in Xanadu, what his luve was like, the spacious firmament on high, or how a drowsy numbness pained his sense: always tacitly prefixing that address O reader! The poet appeared to be talking to somebody he could see — and the mind's eye is as real if not realer than the body's.

At the same time, of course, there has always gone along with this the poet talking to himself, thinking out loud and often in the same poem that employs direct address. Non-vocative poetry is thought-poetry; it is thinking instead of talking, or singing, or in Frost's phrase telling a poem. It is a sort of memorandum from I to me: I thank whatever gods may be/For my unconquerable soul; The paths of glory lead but to the grave; Time present and time past/Are both perhaps present in time future. For hundreds of years the public, because it liked poetry and accepted the poets as odd but astute brethren, thronged to eavesdrop on the poet when he was thinking out loud. Insofar as his thoughts were universal, the public could identify with them and exclaim, Ah! How true! The relationship between public and poet was like that of mind and voice; the mind could not know what it thought till the voice said it. (Many people have the experience of not knowing what they think of, let us say, a picture, until they voice an opinion, which they then recognize as being their own.) Poets like Keats and Shakespeare again and again broke forth the light that the public mind had been groping for in darkness.

But times have changed. If the public does not accept the poet as a more articulate brother, certainly the poet does not accept the public either: he calls it enemy. The public is no longer an eagerly eavesdropping audience. The poetry of thought can and does still speak to many, but to the friends of poetry, not to its foes. The breach between poet and public seems to me to be in the imagination: if the movie star or the intuitive dictator has taken the place of the poet in the public fancy, so has the uncouth movie world or the totalitarian state come to represent the public in the poet's fancy. It is about how awful the public is that he mumbles to himself.

There is, of course, nothing wrong intellectually, morally, or artistically about looking at and talking to oneself. Tocqueville once said that democratic man is "habitually engaged in

the contemplation of a very puny object: namely himself."
Talking to oneself, one can sometimes reach great conclusions,
achieve mystic heights, perhaps come to know one's self. There
is nothing wrong with communicating with one's self except
that it is not communicating with others. And as W. H. Auden
says, "Behind the work of any creative artist is the desire to
communicate his perceptions to others. Those who have no
interest in communication do not become artists; they become
mystics or madmen." To be an artist, it is not enough to perceive something, whether in the external world of sense or the
internal world of feeling; it is not enough, out of perceptions,
to make a thing, a real thing, a poem. If one *is* an artist, the
tension is too great to stop there. It is necessary to complete the
cycle with that curious, trusting, tentative, doubtful act which
consists of an offering of, a hoping for, a waiting to see if.

What I am circling around saying is that it is for the artist
to be generous enough, magnanimous enough, brave enough,
superior enough to be the one who heals the breach. He must
be the one that sacrifices the sitting huddled in his skin, under-
water, eyes closed, breath held, mind-going-like-sixty, to create
something in whose defense he gets angry because nobody in
today's world has truly understood it. It is true that the world
is brutal and obtuse. It is true that it is opposed on every
score to what the poet stands for. It is true that it is not the
poet's friend. But there is the possibility, I should hope, of
communicating with one's enemies as well as with one's friends.
John Ciardi says, "It is my friend in me/That lets me see my
friend." How about the enemy in me? He certainly cannot be
seen clearly enough to be directly addressed. It might be the
ticket, in tracking him down, if I could use the enemy-public

as his surrogate. The sixth book of the Bhagavad-Gita says, "Soul is Self's friend when Self doth rule o'er Self,/But Self turns enemy if Soul's own self/Hates Self as not itself." Could it be that the public is not quite what the poet sees it as? Would it be possible ever to say, It is my foe in me/That lets me see my foe?

For a writer, of whatever kind, to expect agreement from the reader is not merely naïve; it is taking all the fun out of a certain kind of challenge — namely, to see if you can get people to pay attention to what they are not ordinarily interested in, against their own prejudices, even against their conditioning. Such a feat has all the excitement of a leading-astray of the godly, a flashing of strange lights before prim eyes. If I, through a short story, can make an Episcopalian deaconess understand what was felt by a young girl swept off her feet by passion for an Irish riding-master — and feel it, not with her intelligence, but in the way the girl herself experienced it — that's communication. To my way of thinking, communication doesn't mean the agreement of two like-minded souls, or the admiration of a lesser for a greater mind. It is the conveying of an idea, a feeling, an emotion, against stubborn obstacles, and in spite of them; like that courage-to-be which operates in spite of anxiety. Communication is communication only when it is thrown across a void. Then it can be a victory, or the light shining in darkness when suddenly the darkness comprehendeth it.

Certainly the poet will not communicate with an enemy world if he turns his back on it; if he will neither face it nor speak to it. So much is certain. Perhaps for some it is impossible anyway; but it can be tried, under circumstances more favorable to possibility. These conditions are, I believe, helped by looking at, and talking to. Not talking down to; talking *to*. It is amazing how much you can get someone to understand if you look at them. My Georgian friend communicated just fine with those brats whom he'd disliked at sight.

When the poet stands on the near side of the chasm and regards those winding up the face of the cliff to their doom, he can address them in tones that are pitched to reach their ears, even if it is not more than Look out! that he cries. Great sounds have come of such a stance, and may still come, whether in low, confiding tones, as "Whose woods these are I think I know," which certainly is not said to the same self as that speaking. Or chantingly, as "Now as I was young and easy under the apple boughs"; or thrillingly, as "What does it say over the door of Heaven/But *homo fecit?*" Or else in one great burst that brings poet and public, speaker and spoken to, not merely into communication but into one — "O body swayed to music, O brightening glance,/How can we know the dancer from the dance?"

Whatever else these particular modern poems have in common, they have this: they look at some other person, some other self, and they address some other person, some other self, whether friend or foe; if only because, to the great poets who wrote them, it would have been mysticism or madness not to.

{ *FOURTEEN* }

❦

Through the Dark Glass to Reality

ONE OF THE comments people are fond of making to a
writer is, "I read the book you wrote about your childhood," or, "your marriage," or, "your father." Replying to this
remark is difficult. The reader appears to be entirely confident
that his question is based on fact; the fact that this book he
read is about a childhood, or a marriage, or a father; and hence,
it follows, about the writer's own. He is thus one up on the
writer, who is by no means so sure what it is that he was
writing about. *Was* it his own childhood? Perhaps; the novel
certainly contained some of the same scenery and characters.
Was it his marriage? The wife in the novel is annoying enough
to have been his own. Was it his father that he wrote about?
The author did employ quantities of those old, familiar pater-
nal locutions that he can hear forever in his mind's ear.

And yet the writer knows deeply, privately, and absolutely
that what he was writing about was not exactly anything that
ever happened, in his life or anybody else's. It was like reality;

Given as a 1958 William Vaughan Moody Lecture at the University of
Chicago.

{ 225 }

but it was not reality. (No one knows so well as the artist that nothing but reality is reality.) No one but the writer will ever be entirely convinced that even if he had wanted to, he did not, would not, could not put the real world into a work of fiction. Another sort of reality is there. But the fact is that his novel was laid, not in the real world, but in what I have often found it convenient to call the territory of fiction — a quite different, but perfectly definite place.

Persons who find themselves temperamentally unsympathetic to fiction are likely to suspect the very existence of such a territory. Why believe in any such secondary reality — such an anti-reality, to transport the physicists' term? What's the matter with good old primary reality — the one we can see, hear, touch; and furthermore use for reading a roman à clef?

Yet there are to be found, between covers, many clear descriptions of this territory where the only rules are those of fiction. If we study these descriptions carefully enough we may emerge with some idea of where this territory, the world of artistic reality, lies. It is certainly on the other side of the looking-glass; white rabbits in kid gloves, enraged Duchesses with squalling brats, and frog footmen are everyday sights along its paths. Fairyland is one of its names. The *Arabian Nights* describes it in detail. On the other hand, it is not a purely fantastic region, for on its quite humdrum streets walk such prosaic persons as Jane Eyre, Emma Woodhouse, Rawdon Crawley, and Mrs. Moore. It is far from being a heaven, but it is' not hell; it is rather, perhaps, like the land which throve before the coming of Christianity with its Heaven and Hell; it is the land of heart's desire. As a matter of fact Yeats, in his early play of that name, gives one of the clearest descriptions on record of the nature and characteristics of this territory of which we are speaking.

Into this world, out of a sometimes harsh and always demanding outer reality, the writer escapes with cries of joy and relief. And not only the writer. For let us recognize that to an army of readers as well, the territory of fiction is a beloved and welcome retreat from what is sometimes known as real life. Anyone who has ever responded to the first lines of certain great novels — beginnings that seem to swing apart like gates — has been there. They are the reader's Open Sesame to this world of anti-reality. Let me reprint a few such opening lines.

"It is a truth universally acknowledged, that a single man in possession of a good fortune must be in want of a wife."

And another:

"Happy families are all alike; every unhappy family is unhappy in its own way."

And another:

"For a long time I used to go to bed early. Sometimes, when I had put out my candle, my eyes would close so quickly that I had not even time to say, 'I'm going to sleep.' "

And still another:

"That old bell, presage of a train, had just sounded through Oxford station; and the undergraduates who were waiting there, gay figures in tweed or flannel, moved to the margin of the platform and gazed idly up the line."

And — for I hate to give up this opening of doors upon delicious worlds beyond — one more:

"I wish either my father or my mother, or indeed both of them, as they were in duty equally bound to it, had minded what they were about when they begot me. . . . "

But since I see that this first sentence of what might *appear* to be an autobiographical novel is going to run to twenty-nine lines, I must stop.

All I have been trying to do is to bring back the sensation the reader had when he opened the sort of book that can lead straight out of this world, into another. A young writer who, by his own account, had traveled a lot in that other, golden realm, described the sensation on first looking into a certain kind of book, in words which are ultimate.

The truth is that there are two realities. What I would like to consider here is the relationship between the two. There must *be* a relationship. As the Hindus would say, the fact that there are two posits a relationship. I would like to consider this relationship in the light of its bearing upon the autobiographical element in fiction.

An autobiographical element of course exists. The writer is, more or less, bound to his own experience. Even ogres, even unicorns and Djinns, can only be imagined in terms of their likeness to, or difference from, existing creatures. The writer's creative phantasies mount, like balloons, up from the low-lying marshes of memory itself. The writer works with what other people forget. It appears that he cannot forget. He fans the spark left in memory, to bring beauty from its ashes. Now it is characteristic of memory, as a mode of thinking, that, first, it is essentially unreliable, and that, second, it tends to burst spontaneously into phantasy, that is to say, imagining. It is the imagination thus conceived that opens the door for the writer into the other world, the territory of fiction, the land of heart's desire. Three questions present themselves to us: What makes this happen to the writer? How does the writer function in that world of imagination? and How does he get out again?

Freud has answered these questions, for those seeking a psychological explanation, in two sentences: "If the individual who is displeased with reality is in possession of that artistic talent which is still a psychological riddle, he can transform his phantasies into artistic creations. So he escapes the fate of a neurosis and wins back his connection by this roundabout way." Freud here gives *phantasy* its psychological meaning of daydreaming.

While, with his inimitable map-making faculty, Freud has thus laid down a pattern, he has not really explained the artist in terms of the artist's experience. Much as the Apostles' Creed lays down a pattern of Christian dynamics, Freud has merely established that the artist is displeased with reality; that he possesses a mysterious talent which enables him to transform phantasies into creations; and that he can by doing so win back his connection with reality. But just as the Creed skirts the actual life of its subject, so Freud avoids a definition of the factor that sets his whole pattern in motion — the artistic talent which, he confesses, remains a riddle. I should not dream of rushing in with definitions where Freud feared to tread. But I suggest that by listening very carefully to a number of writers of widely varied talents — by listening not only for what they say but for what sneaks past them when they are inattentive — and by trying to visualize the images, as well as hear what goes on, we may emerge with a closer, or at least a more felt, understanding of the relationship between the real and the fictional worlds.

We can already assert one thing about that relationship. I think we have seen how the door which is the writer's own memory leads, by way of imagination, into fiction. We might say that the writer is, in himself, a sort of door, or passage, that leads from the real world into the fictional one. Whether the door leads out again is another thing.

From ancient myth straight through to modern fiction, the various aspects of the artist's special relation to the world of imagination are pictured again and again, whether in overt terms or in concealed images, in symbols. *What makes this happen to the artist?* You will remember that when the Fisherman in the *Arabian Nights* had three times cast his nets fruitlessly, he cast them once more and brought up in them, not fish, but a bottle of brass, its mouth sealed with a lead stopper bearing the seal of King Solomon the Wise. He realized that it would be the bright thing, the realistic thing, to sell the bottle at the marketplace for ten pieces of gold. But our Fisherman was one of those dissatisfied with reality. He had to pick the stopper out of the bottle to see what was inside. As you know, out came a monstrous Djinn "whose head was in the clouds while his feet rested upon the earth; with hands like winnowing forks and legs like masts; nostrils like trumpets and eyes like lamps," a very epitome of unleashed psychic energy, and furthermore bent upon destroying the Fisherman. Most of the rest of the story is devoted to the desperate expedients the Fisherman must go to to get that Djinn he so rashly let out of the bottle back into it.

We don't have to look very far to find examples in modern fiction of this theme of the escape of the artist's energy, his *élan vital,* from the container that everyday reality provides for it. There are the innumerable fictional children who feel *different* from other children. There are characters like Heathcliff, Levin, Pierre in *War and Peace,* Jane Eyre, Raskolnikov; the unwanted, the rejected, the obsessed, the inferior; the, in any case, alienated. For it doesn't really signify whether the character rejects society or it rejects him. The artist's sense of alienation is often to be found projected onto the real world; to him it can appear less as if he were displeased with reality than as if reality were displeased with him.

I am going to analyze a short story of my own as an example of this aspect of alienation. My story is typical of so-called autobiographical fiction, and I ought to be in an excellent position to tell you how much of it is, and how much isn't, actually autobiographical.

Although the writer's phantasies originate in what he cannot forget, it would be a mistake to suppose that this means he can dig for and find the material of his fictions in the past. Rather, it comes *to* him, transmuted, somewhere out of sight and mind, into the form of an idea.

The subject that, then, came to me for the story called "The Empress's Ring," I chose to write in the first person, and I shall tell it now in the first person. As a little girl I am given a tiny gold ring set with five turquoises, which once belonged to the Empress of Austria — the beautiful Elisabeth, who used to climb mountains. It is to me an unbelievably precious possession, all the more so since everything else I have seems to be inferior to the possessions of Mimi, the little girl with naturally curly hair who lives next door, who has a beautiful new playhouse and new doll's china with pink rosebuds on it. But now I own the ring of an Empress, and it is beautiful and I love it and all is changed. I wear it when I go out to play, disregarding all warnings, since it is far too precious ever to get lost. But then I do lose it, in the sand of my messy, scattered sandpile, which is also inferior to Mimi's sandpile. At first I am hardly dismayed, since I know it is still there, somewhere within a circumscribed area. I am sure that all I have to do is dig for it and find it. But I never do find it, although for years I try; and when I have become a young lady going to dances I sometimes remember suddenly the unbearable loss of my little ring, the one with the five turquoises in it, and go out in my chic beige dress and my high heels and dig in the sand of the abandoned sandpile for it. Now, the story goes on, I am a middle-aged woman, and live in another part of the country. Today I went out as usual to take a walk, and passed the house of some neighbors whom I am rather in awe of since their house is much nicer than mine, their silver is always well polished, and their slipcovers, unlike mine, always seem to fit. I would like to stop and see them, but I let shyness get the better of me and go on home. When I am indoors again I stop for a moment's rest on the sofa. Let me quote a bit from the ending: "I lay down, and as soon as I closed my eyes there I was again, years and years later, back in the old woodshed of the place where I grew up, scratching and clawing at the sandpile, trying to find my little blue ring."

This story certainly sounds autobiographical, and it is usually taken by readers to be autobiographical. In fact it *felt* autobiographical while I was writing it. I could see the sun glinting on the five blue stones of my little gold ring as I went out to play; I could visualize the fortunate Mimi with her fat curls. It was with almost a shock, therefore, that much later it dawned on me that I had never, in fact, been given a ring that belonged to the Empress of Austria or any other Empress; and that the only ring I ever did own as a child, I never lost, in the sandpile or anywhere else. If I try to explain this to one of the kind readers who condole with me over this poignant childhood loss of mine, they tend to look suspicious and offended, as though they thought I might be rejecting their sympathy. For the story apparently carries the ring of truth.

I think there is another kind of truth in it, one which we may find pertinent to our consideration of the first aspect of the artist's special experience, that of alienation. This truth was partly expressed by a reader in Canada who wrote me about "The Empress's Ring." He said, "I too lost a precious possession when I was a child — the little pearl-handled knife my father had given me for my birthday. I know how you felt about the loss of your ring, and I know, too, that you are only calling it a ring."

If it is not a ring that the little girl in the story lost, what is it? A ring is a symbol of connection, of the closed circuit, of both narcissism and wholeness. This only occurred to me long after the story was published. (Only afterwards, usually long afterwards, do I become aware of the symbols in my work, and I think this is a general experience with writers.) This ring of connectedness, then, that had been given to the little girl in the story, was lost in the sand. It was not destroyed, for it is there somewhere if the little girl, who becomes a woman, still with the same sense of inferiority, could only find it again.

Now there is no more alienating force than a sense of inferiority. It negates both self and society, by placing them in a false relation with each other. The little girl in the story is one of those whom Freud describes as displeased with reality — in this case, with the reality of herself as a person; her own sense of integrity is lost deep in the sandy shifting contents of childhood. For it would be a grave mistake to suppose that the reality from which the artist is alienated is necessarily the reality of other people. Charity begins at home, and so does self-rejection.

Having become displeased with reality, having been alienated from his true self and hence from the real world, having once let the Djinn of psychic energy out of the circular jar which properly contained it, the artist is nevertheless not at the end of his rope. *How does the artist function, in the world of imagination?* The artist is one who, although alienated, can still communicate. Upon that ability to communicate rests much. Readers who today complain of their inability to follow, to enjoy, or to understand what modern poets are saying are in no more unfortunate a case than the poets themselves, their lines of communication down. Happy the artist who has a firm idea of the thousand things he wants to say, is learning more and more to know how to say them well, and has a body of readers, however small, who can follow, enjoy, and at least in part understand what he says. He is happy, and he is lord of the territory of fiction, where he can king it, having once entered by means of the magic password Open Sesame.

There, like Ali Baba, he stands. This second stage of the artist's relation to artistic reality is to be compared with what Freud called "that artistic talent which is still a psychological riddle." At the same time that the artist's ring of wholeness disappeared into the shifting sands, he received the gift of that password which has let him into the wonderland where he now stands. Sacks of rubies and emeralds, of ideas and images and fancies, spill their contents for him on every hand. In fact, he seems to have gained considerably by the exchange. The artist is, today, highly thought of, not only by himself but by society. He has achieved possessions greatly in excess of that one little gold ring; riches which may be balanced against what Freud calls the normal aims of the ego — honor, riches, and the love of women. What honors, what women will he not be able to obtain with the wealth that has been opened to him by the application of the words Open Sesame? We might observe in passing that sesame is an East Indian seed, and recall the Christian promise that if one's faith is even as a grain of mustard seed it will remove mountains. The kind of seed they use in the *Arabian Nights,* that is to say, in the territory of fiction, can open up caves filled with the ill-gotten gains of the Forty Thieves. What price mountain removal?

The subject of great power has always been a favorite in fiction. Dumas' *Count of Monte Cristo* describes it, Tolstoi's character of Napoleon in *War and Peace* studies it, and there has appeared in recent years, through science fiction, the increasingly intriguing theme of man's conquest of space. At the moment we have the artist shut away from outer reality in the cave of precious jewels and ideas, of phantasy. Science fiction surely still offers us a field as far removed from autobiographical experience as we are likely to find. Let us examine a specimen of it to see whether it is in fact as objectively imagined and as unrelated to its author's personal problems and memories as would appear.

E. M. Forster's story "The Machine Stops," a forerunner of the science fiction genre, is laid at some far distant point in time. Civilization is found to have moved into the interior of the earth, which is honeycombed with individual cells, one for each member of this unsocial society. The cells are furnished with every sort of pushbutton device for the occupant's private necessities, luxury, education, and entertainment. This system of living is entirely dependent upon the Machine, which is the central and prime cause of continued existence under these artificial circumstances. By the time the story opens, the Machine has come actually to be worshiped by the inhabitants of the honeycomb; what was once the book of instructions is now venerated as a Bible. It is quite in order that the members of this civilization no longer have any hair or teeth; such growths are considered disgusting when they are occasionally encountered, in the few beings left who have not properly adjusted to the Machine. The protagonist of the story is a woman, content to live in her cell pursuing what is considered the most desirable of all aims, "having ideas." But her son, who lives at the opposite side of the globe, is filled with inchoate longings to get out on the outside of the earth and see what is there. When he expresses these deviationist desires to his mother, having pressed her into paying him a visit, she is horrified, alarmed, and advises him strongly against them. She is only too eager to return to her snug solitude to have more ideas. But the son does struggle to the surface of the earth, and although human lungs are by now unfit to breathe natural air with ease, he does draw in a few breaths of outside freedom before he is pulled back, horribly, by the wormlike devices devised by the Machine for such emergencies.

Soon after, something inconceivable begins: the Machine itself starts to fail. At first nobody grasps such an impossibility. But the Machine goes on slowly failing, for it is only a machine and not, as its dependents have come to think, God. From having venerated the book of instructions too long, nobody knows how to fix it. The air goes bad, the communication ceases, and the walls begin to crumble, bringing complete destruction to those who have relied on the Machine for everything. In the end mother and son, reunited at the moment of ultimate catastrophe, look up through ghastly, rending, toppling ruins and see, far above, what has been there all along: the real stars in the real sky.

In this frightening tale, we may relate the civilization within the interior of the earth to the inner world of imagination of which we have been speaking. The monstrous Machine which keeps everything going is to be equated with the mechanism of imagination itself. For imagination is not a proper function of cognition, which in any way relates the individual to the real world, but a subjective mechanism, dealing entirely with self-generated, self-determined, self-regarding phantasies. It is easy to identify the denizens of Forster's interior world, dependent for everything upon this wish-fulfilling Machine, and worshiping it, with the artists, critics, persons of every sort who worshp imagination and believe art — the creation of ideas — to be an end in itself for which the real world, the outside of the planet with its harsh atmosphere, is well lost. This is the stagnant art life of which Elinor Wylie wrote:

> O virtuous light, if thou be man's
> Or matter of the meteor stone,

Prevail against this radiance
Which is engendered of its own!

In that unnatural existence a mother was satisfied to be half a world away from her son and merely irritated when his appeal takes her away from her delightfully cerebral pursuits. Now, mother and child make up a universal image, one which expresses as well as the mind can grasp the concept of love. Long ago Yeats pointed out that there is no love in the land of heart's desire. There is no love in Forster's interior civilization. That too is what is wrong with the treasure-filled cave of Ali Baba. The gold and pearls and gems are cold and lifeless; and when Ali Baba's brother Cassim forgets the password and finds himself trapped in the cave, the riches turn to bitterness and mockery as he hears the approach of the robbers who will destroy him.

While I don't mean for a moment to go poking about in the austere mansions of Mr. Forster's private life, I think we can see, without laboring the point, what was in the mind of the distinguished Cambridge don, the artist of *Howards End* and *A Passage to India,* the celebrant, in a dozen short stories, of life and love as higher than thought. While "The Machine Stops" certainly cannot be called factually autobiographical, neither is it the objective and unrelated phantasy of the world a million years from now that we might have supposed. In fact we are perhaps ready to ask, in the light of Forster's illuminating reverie, is *any* phantasy objective? Is not all phantasy subjectively oriented? Is not, in fact, the world of phantasy — what we have called the territory of fiction — for all its vast treasure, its delights and marvels — in another of its aspects a sealed cave, an airless internal world dependent upon a

{ 238 }

monstrous machine that must fail ultimately, a mere version of egotism? To quote the same Wylie poem:

This light engendered of itself
Is not a light by which to live.

Perhaps the artist might be content enough to get along without human love, but unfortunately, trapped within his wonderland, he hears the robbers coming to kill him; the Djinn of power whom he let out of the bottle darkens the whole sky, breathing out the death which all myth, all legend, all prophecy postulates as the concomitant of lovelessness. It appears that whether he is interested in love or not, the artist has to take it into account or perish. To put all this in different terms, the aims and the standards of art are, quite simply, perfection; but perfection, while very nice indeed in its place, is incompatible with a real world whose very imperfections are what causes love to operate. He who, when we first investigated him, was displeased with reality, is now displeased with unreality also. *How can the writer get out again?*

Realizing the negative and destructive aspects of the enchanting country to which he has given his allegiance is surely the artist's lowest moment. Katherine Mansfield, a spokesman for all the writers who ever tried to reconcile reality with phantasy, imagination with truth, wrote toward the end of her life when she was absorbed with the problem of integrity, "One heard, in one's own being, 'I have missed it. I have given up. This is not what I want. If this is all, then Life is not worth living.' [I] have led, ever since [I] can remember, a very typically false life. Yet, through it all, there have been moments . . . Life should be like a steady, visible light."

It is clear that the conflicting claims of the two worlds, the real and the fictional, are only to be settled by uniting them in some way. Of course in actual fact they *are* one. Forster's globe had an outside as well as an inside, although nobody went to it. Outside the cave of Ali Baba, all the time, is the real world, full of humanity and imperfection and suffering and love. It would seem that the only thing separating them is that door which will swing apart only to Open Sesame, that door which as we have seen *is* the artist. It would seem that nothing cuts the artist off from reality but himself; no annihilation threatens him but his own other side.

When Sultan Shahriyar, convinced of the infidelity of all women, took to marrying a new bride each night and having her executed in the morning, the lovely Scheherazade managed to outwit her doom by telling such enthralling tales that the Sultan could not bear to destroy the source of his entertainment. So she survived for a thousand nights and a night. The writer, too, whose creativity, symbolized by the feminine side of his nature, has also rejected fidelity to the reality which the death-dealing sultan represents, may also stave off a fatal severing by continuing to tell stories. Thus, as Freud said, he escapes the fate of a neurosis, or psychological death, and transforms his phantasies into artistic creations. Certainly there are many writers who write as if their life depended upon it.

Such are the compulsive writers. These are the writers who, in every book, repeat, with variations, the same unsolved problem over and over: the Eugene Gant or George Webber of Wolfe, Marquand's small-town boy suffering from inferiority in the great world; the recurrent abused child in Dickens, who represents what Edmund Wilson calls the wound. Are these novels to be called autobiographical? Not in detail, often; not in plot; but their problems are the problems, unconscious and unfaced, of their authors.

The sufferings of Katherine Mansfield, both physical and spiritual, were such that one can hardly bear to speak of them. However, her torment, torn between her dedication to art, her struggle with tuberculosis and heart trouble, the frustration of her passion for Middleton Murry, is today so familiar to readers as to need no dwelling on. What has received less attention is the fact that in her last years, as she approached a crisis of the spirit, a yearning after purgation and rebirth, she turned more and more to what may be called autobiographical themes. One exquisite story followed another that evoked the New Zealand of her childhood, charged with beauty, quivering with feeling. Are these to be put down to the nostalgia for one's childhood that might accompany disease of the lungs and impending death? Are they simply a further turning away from real life to the world of art?

I think that if the reader will listen with a sensitive ear to such late stories as "At the Bay" and "Prelude," he will hear Katherine Mansfield again and again spell out the nature of her psychological predicament, and even make suggestions for its solution. For if it is the artist's own imagination which leads him astray from reality, it is also imagination which prefigures the way back. One gets the impression of Katherine Mansfield looking in her childhood for something lost, and finding it. I cannot believe that she was conscious of these signposts which her creativity erected to guide her. Her last

days, at the Gurdjieff Institute in Fontainebleau, when she
sought to take the kingdom of heaven by storm, seem to me
to preclude the possibility that she saw any other way.

Let us examine, briefly, the beautiful story "Prelude." Mansfield's biographer, Anthony Alpers, who has elsewhere much
of value to contribute concerning his subject, gives us here the
conventionally sympathetic view of what "Prelude" is about. I
quote: " 'Prelude' is simply a picture of a New Zealand family
moving from a house in town and settling in another in the
country. It has no plot, in the sense of a prearranged scheme of
causes and effects requiring to be followed to conclusions; it
only sets out to show what the people of the household think
and feel, and how they behave as they adjust themselves to the
new home. It shows them realizing, in their different ways, how
their lives are going to be subtly altered by their new sur-
roundings. When it has done this, it stops."

I contend that "Prelude" does and says infinitely more than
this, and furthermore in terms of deeply felt cause and effect,
requiring to be followed to a conclusion. A biographer should
be interested in this conclusion, since it is the pass to which
Katherine Mansfield's overworked sensibility had brought her.
At the very beginning of the story we are given a clue; the
mother, Linda Burnell, looks at the bags and boxes piled on
the floor of the buggy that will drive her to the new house.
" 'These are absolute necessities,' she said, her voice trembling
with fatigue and excitement." The two little girls, who are not
to be taken along on this trip, hear her. One of them is Kezia,
who has been generally identified with the child Katherine
Mansfield once was. "Hand in hand they stared with round
solemn eyes, first at the absolute necessities and then at their

mother." Kezia is a little girl, then, who in competition with bags and boxes for importance to her mother came second.

This theme, the lack of love from mother to child, is stressed over and over as the story proceeds. Linda Burnell is too tired from child-bearing, too exhausted by the demands of her bumbling and importunate husband, to give her children love. "I wish you would go out into the garden and give an eye to your children," old Mrs. Fairfield, the grandmother, says. "But that I know you will not do." Only the grandmother, a representative of the past, has love to give. Katherine Mansfield shows Linda herself thinking of the importance of love: "There was something comforting in the sight of her own mother that Linda felt she could never do without. She needed the sweet smell of her flesh, and the soft feel of her cheeks . . ." But this is not Linda loving; this is Linda wanting love. Linda Burnell is described as being remarkably like the ill Katherine Mansfield. And it would be a mistake to imagine that because Kezia represents the childhood Katherine Mansfield, she is the only character in the story who, so to speak, *is* Katherine Mansfield. Other aspects of her needs, her lacks, her dilemma are to be found in every feminine character in the story. And of course, to more or less degree, all characters are and must be projections of their author. Katherine Mansfield could not tell us what her real mother really thought, all those years ago; Linda's thoughts are her own thoughts. It seems to me that Linda, the ailing mother, expresses the feeling part of Katherine Mansfield that had turned entirely to phantasy; her sick self. Some of the most fascinating passages in the story deal with Linda's imaginings as she turns her face to the wall, lying in bed, and traces a poppy in the wallpaper with her finger.

"She could feel the sticky, silky petals, the stem, hairy like a gooseberry skin, the rough leaf and tightly glazed bud. Things had a habit of coming alive like that."

Linda and Kezia are brought together alone once in the story, at the site of the monstrous aloe that grows in front of the house, "with its cruel leaves and fleshy stem. The curving leaves seemed to be hiding something; the blind stem cut into the air as if no wind could ever shake it. 'Does it ever have any flowers?' " the little girl asks her mother, and Linda replies, " 'Once every hundred years.' "

Let us pause to examine this aloe, the most important symbol in a story full of important objects. Katherine Mansfield's title for the first version of this story was "The Aloe." The description she gives of the plant is repellent. Yet Linda Burnell — who is always having phantasies of going away and leaving this great exhausting crew of a family — looks at the aloe, later, in the moonlight, and "Her heart grew hard. She particularly liked the long sharp thorns." Nobody would dare to bother her, she thinks, if she were like that; not even her husband. "He was too strong for her," she thought now. "She had always hated things that rushed at her, from a child. There were times when . . . [Burnell] was frightening. When she just had not screamed at the top of her voice: 'You are killing me.' And at those times she had longed to say the most coarse, hateful things." But of course Linda never had. If all the masculine characters in "Prelude" are crude and insensate, all the feminine characters are submissive to them, even the old grandmother.

"Prelude" was written shortly after the drastic shock of the death of Katherine Mansfield's beloved younger brother; and it is my belief that her urge to write a story about the move to a new house reveals the awareness of a necessity to begin her own life on a new footing, to face inner facts and make a fresh start. The aloe stands directly in front of the new house, where you can't miss it. It seems to me that in this thorny growth we see embodied the self-protective, loveless ego that cerebral preoccupations produce, comparable to Forster's airless interior world. Certainly Katherine Mansfield, in the days before her death, spoke often with horror of the purely cerebral life. She never describes the loveless condition so brutally as when she draws the aloe.

But in "Prelude" there is another, positive aspect to the thorny aloe. If Linda Burnell were more like that aloe, she thinks, she would be strong; strong enough, we may add, to love Kezia. And the grandmother says that there are signs that the aloe may blossom, this year.

What does this mean? I think it suggests that, rare though it be, the aloe of egotism and self-enclosure *is* capable of a flowering. Such a flowering would make the aloe acceptable to these flower-loving, feminine characters, thus bridging the gap between the cerebral and the instinctive.

If love is that which connects, then its absence means a gap. Both Linda and Kezia, the unloved little girl, are conscious of a division that shows itself in the projection of a mysterious and vaguely masculine They, of whom Linda thinks, "*They* knew how frightened she was. . . . What Linda always felt was that *They* wanted something of her, and she knew if she gave herself up and was quiet . . . something would really happen." The split is more definitely dealt with near the end of the story when Beryl, the vain young sister who gives us an explanatory self-consciousness, is berating herself for being divided between falseness and what she feels to be true in her. "Life is rich and mysterious and good, and I am rich and mysterious and good, too. Shall I ever be that Beryl for ever? . . . How can I? And was there ever a time when I did not have a false self?"

As if in answer, the door opens and little Kezia comes in. She is the answer to the problem of the split. She has feeling, not for phantasies, but for reality, the niceness of the man who drives the dray, the colors of real flowers in the garden. And she needs more than anything to be loved — that is, nurtured, cultivated. This is the message I believe Katherine Mansfield's imagination sent to her about herself through "Prelude."

"Prelude" was followed by the equally beautiful story "At the Bay," also dealing with scenes from Katherine Mansfield's childhood. But the preoccupation is no longer with the feminine side of the Burnell ménage. "At the Bay" is about men. These men are all at once seen, not as brutal, but as touching, fumbling, and eager. A new character is introduced, an artistic brother-in-law, in whom Linda's escape impulses are now lodged. And something has been born, just as "Prelude" prophesied: there is a new baby boy. Man has always been the symbol of woman's reality, a baby boy is a symbol of a new reality, and it is almost uncanny to see that *something*, which led Katherine Mansfield to present her inner needs in "Prelude," giving the answer to them in "At the Bay." But Katherine Mansfield herself, determined to find what she called purity of vision, died of a tubercular hemorrhage in Fontainebleau. On the day of her death, Murry wrote, she seemed "a being transfigured by love." She knew that love is the flowering of the aloe. Yet the artist is one who knows more than he can apply.

Fiction is an artistically controlled personal myth, which, in its coming together into a form, releases more or less overtones of the universal. In both these aspects it can be said to have a value that exists in the world of reality — its value to the world as a work of art, and its value, realized or not, to the artist. If, seen negatively, all phantasy is self-regarding, so, affirmatively speaking, phantasy, fiction, bears upon the conscious personality of its creator to compensate it, criticizing and supplementing it.

The territory of fiction is thus the other half of the world of reality: the dark side of the moon, the mantelpiece mirror that reflects the chamber, the dream between the wakings, the shadow within the sunlight. If there is an Open Sesame of talent to let the artist in to the world of imagination, there is a password of understanding to let him out again, into a reality which he has, perhaps, come to value also.

After the thousand and one nights' entertainment, the Sultan relented and freed Scheherazade from the threat of death. The Sultan is also a part of the artist. For even though the artist was displeased with his reality, he could never escape it; it was there, threatening him. Sultan and Scheherazade are thus one more image of the two sides that make up a totality out of the real world and its lovely consort, fiction.

Children always ask after a story is finished, What happened next? After she was pardoned, didn't Scheherazade ever tell any more tales of Djinns and rocs' eggs and cities of brass? Have no fear. I am sure that, released from the danger of death, Scheherazade could always tell a good story when she put her mind to it.